CW01659222

DOMII

THE ULTIMATE PET BUSINESS PLAN

How to launch, grow and scale an outrageously profitable, impactful and fun pet business that dominates your local town

Published by

www.elitepublishingacademy.com

All rights reserved.

No part of this book may be reproduced in any form by photocopying or any electronic or mechanical means, including information storage or retrieval systems, without permissions in writing from both the copyright owner and the publisher of the book.

First Edition published 2019
© Dominic Hodgson

Printed and bound in Great Britain by
www.elitepublishingacademy.com

A catalogue record for this book
is available from The British Library
ISBN
978-1-912713-78-3

Praise for *The Ultimate Pet Business Plan*

What pet professionals are saying about *The Ultimate Pet Business Plan*

"This is my new favourite book for dog business owners. Dom has taken the key points for success and not only applied them to our industry but made them easy to understand in his signature style.

Anyone looking to break out of the 'starving dog trainer/walker/groomer' mould and treat their business with the respect it deserves should start with *The Ultimate Pet Business Plan*."

Nick Benger
Dog Trainer and Podcast Host
www.nickbenger.com

"This book literally gives you the Ultimate Pet Business Plan that will guide you through starting up a new pet business, increasing your profits, growing your business and branching out.

Having read this book it has now become my business bible. It's enjoyable to read, it's easy to navigate through and it's full of some cracking ideas and brilliant free resources. I will be constantly referring to this book to help keep my business on track as it grows. My business is established but I've taken away a lot from this book and it has helped me to refocus."

Sally Cousins
Dog Walker
www.wooferswalkies.com

"They say if you want to learn something, then go to someone who is where you want to be. Or who has been on the journey you see yourself going on. Who has made the mistakes so you don't have to …

This is what Dominic does in this book. It's step-by-step, straight-talking advice that is easy to follow.

If you're thinking of setting up a pet business, this will take away all the overwhelm you might be feeling.

If you already have a pet business and are fed up of the constant stream of people telling you all the things you should be doing and feel frazzled and exhausted, give yourself half a day off to read this book.

Sometimes we all need to take a step back and reset, to try something different, and if you haven't tried Dominic's methods, look at his testimonials for reassurance that they do work.

This book will give you clarity, focus and actionable steps to follow and is a must for petpreneurs."

Rachel Spencer
Pet Business Blogging and Media Coach
www.publicityforpetbusinesses.co.uk

"Help more people, earn more money and have an impact? 'No thanks!' … said no one ever.

As one of his private coaching clients, Dom has been hammering into me a lot recently my business's leadership status. 'Great,' I thought smugly, 'I'll skim-read phase one and two. Phase three is where I'm at.' An hour later I was still making notes on the phase one chapters. That's hubris for you.

Even if, like me, your business is quite established, there are still many valuable lessons early on in the book. Fail to implement them at your peril. Having been a Platinum coaching client of Dom's for six months now, and having put many of the Golden Rules Rules into action, I can tell you that it works.

So if you've already solved all of the dog owners' problems in your town, you love every aspect of your business, are getting all of the time off to spend with family and friends that you desire, as well as being able to support that time off financially, this book will be a waste of your time.

Anyone else, read on …"

Katie Guastapaglia
Canine Enrichment Officer – Dogwood Adventure Play
www.dogwoodadventureplay.com

"This is the ultimate business and marketing guide for pet businesses!

In his latest offering, Dom Hodgson takes you by the hand and shows you exactly how to stand out from your competition, build a profitable business, and systemise and grow a successful enterprise that will earn you more than enough cash to live a comfortable life.

Easy-to-follow advice that works, regardless of whether you are just starting out or are an established pet business owner, as long as you put in the work required, of course!"

Natasja Lewis
Dog Trainer
www.nightsabredogtraining.co.uk

"As always, Dom, your stuff is straightforward, and laid out in an easy-to-understand way. This is a cracking little book to help newbies and the clueless (like I used to be!) on their way to a more profitable and customised business!"

Tam Wilson
Born 2 Run Pet Care – Premium Canine Adventures
www.born2runpetcare.com

"Dom has produced another cracker of a book. It does exactly what it says on the tin: 'the ultimate pet business plan'.

Dom writes with so much passion for marketing and shares all his mistakes and wins, successes and failures. There are some laugh-out-loud moments too.

If you can implement all the information from all three phases, your business will be riding high, more profitable and you will be a lot happier."

Harriet Goodall
Dog Walker
www.pawtasticgundogadventures.co.uk

"I love this book! An easy to read, short and to the point, problem-solving packed book with no waffle. Full of useful tips too, it makes the process of building your business easy to understand and follow. The Golden Rules can be applied to any pet business and have made a huge difference to mine already.

As part of Dom's Diamond coaching group in the PBIC, I have worked through all Dom's Golden Rules and continue to do so. I am not a natural salesperson and have always hated being 'pushy' and 'selling', but I now sell Silver, Gold and Ultimate puppy packages much more often than single sessions. It keeps my clients on track with their dogs, and they keep coming back for more.

Following a chat with Dom, I sat and thought hard about my niche as I enjoy all aspects of dog training, but what I love most as a behaviourist/dog trainer is helping fearful and anxious dogs overcome their problems, it is my passion – and so The Happy Dog Project was born. I have an academy, a forum, literature to send out, online client only areas to help them and I am currently writing my book.

I work my ass off but I'm loving every minute of it."

Kerry Lawson
Dog Trainer
www.thefairydogmother.co.uk/hdp

"After reading this book I was left inspired to want to do more with my business. This is a great read with some brilliant advice to help make your business stand out from the competition.

I read this book in one sitting and found it so useful and informative that I couldn't put it down.

A fantastic book with some great advice."

Tim Jackson
Dog Trainer
www.pets2impress.com

"This book is your first step into turning your same as everyone else's pet business into a premium pet business that you can grow. Dom is straight speaking, tells you how it is and doesn't drown you in techno babble; furthermore, he has lived through all the steps too, which is a bonus.

I speak from experience, having followed the steps laid out in the book, and have not looked back. I started my dog walking business, Edinburgh Holistic Dogs, in Feb 2017, and as I write this review I have been in Dom's world a little over 18 months. It's Nov 2019, and I operate in one of the most saturated areas of Edinburgh for professional dog walkers ... new ones popping up all over! However, I don't even care because my walks are full and have been for well over a year. I have a staff member also providing my walks and, oh yeah, I charge 50% more for an hour's walk than everyone else.

In February this year, I launched my dog training services, I created my own packages, charge far more than other trainers in the area and my classes are full. I have been featured in the local press and write my own blog too. Everything Dom has mentioned in this book I have done. Yes, it's hard work, and yes, it's fucking scary as hell, but it is beyond worth it.

The biggest icing on the cake for me is this year I took two weeks' holiday; never ever have I done that before!! Plus I could afford to take that much time away from my business.

Read this book, learn from it and I dare you follow it because you won't regret it. Or you could just remain a sheep like everyone else."

Suzanne Gould
Chief Canine Happiness Officer
www.edinburghholisticdogs.co.uk

The Ultimate Pet Business Plan

A personal note from the author, and special book buyers' bonus

Dear Pet Business Owner,

Thanks for buying my book. You are in for a life-changing experience.

To reward you for investing in your pet business education I have a special bonus that will help you move forward faster with your business growth.

I've recorded an exclusive audio version of this book, which is packed with bonus materials, examples and case studies that back up and verify the proven marketing secrets I share in *The Ultimate Pet Business Plan.*

To get immediate access to this valuable resource, go to:

www.growyourpetbusinessfast.com/resources

Warmly

Dom Hodgson
The Pet Biz Wiz
www.growyourpetbusinessfast.com

Dedication
(that's what you need ...)

The Ultimate Pet Business Plan is dedicated to all the pet professionals I work with in the Pet Business Inner Circle. I believe you are the standard bearers for this industry, and I love helping you make more of an impact with your amazing skills.

Contents

Introduction

Why you need a pet business plan

"A goal without a plan is just a wish"
Antoine de Saint-Exupéry

Three fish lived in a pond. One was named 'Plan ahead', another was 'Think fast' and the third was 'Wait and see'.

Weird names, I know, but work with me here …

One morning they heard a fisherman say he would be casting his net in their pond the next day.

'Plan ahead' said, "I am swimming down the river and heading to the sea tonight."

'Think fast' said, "With my lightning-quick thinking, I'm sure to come up with a plan when I need to."

'Wait and see' lazily said, "I can't be bothered to think about it now."

The next day came around and, sure enough, the fisherman cast his net in the pond.

By this time 'Plan ahead' had already made his way far away from danger and was safe in the ocean.

But 'Think fast' and 'Wait and see' were caught by the fisherman.

True to his name, 'Think fast' quickly rolled onto his belly, went limp, closed his eyes and pretended to be dead. "Bugger, this fish is no good!" said the fisherman and threw him back into the safety of the water.

However, 'Wait and see' was killed and ended up on a plate with some chips and mushy peas.

That is why people say, "In times of danger, when the net is cast, plan ahead or plan to think fast."

A fishy story for sure, but there's a good reason I'm starting this book with a poisson-filled parable.

When starting a new business, or when you are expanding or going in a new direction with an established business, it always pays to plan ahead.

Why you need a business plan

As a business owner you'll find there's always a dangerous net ready to be cast over your operation.

This net takes many forms.

It could be your ever-growing competition who are always hungrily eyeing up your assets as they try to pilfer your customers.

It might be the ever-changing business environment. The pet services sector has undergone some huge changes in the last 10 years, and the next 10 are set to be just as unpredictable.

Or, it could be your own indifference, laziness or lack of imagination which causes your pet business to falter.

Trust me, if you aren't constantly thinking of new ways to promote your services that excite your prospects and thrill your clients, then their head will be turned by someone else.

How to do you prevent this happening to your business?

By planning, of course, and just as importantly, taking action …

The dictionary definition of plan is a detailed proposal for doing or achieving something.

The Ultimate Pet Business Plan will, if you follow it closely, help you to achieve something special. It will enable you to build a pet business that attracts the best clients and to earn a fantastic income, and it will allow you to make a tremendous impact in your canine community.

That last point is worth touching on.

I've had three different businesses within the pet industry, I've written four books on the subject, and I've met and mentored hundreds of passionate pet business owners over the last eight years.

I know you want your business to be the vehicle that brings you and your family everything you deserve.

I also know you aren't in this 'just for the money'. I know you are passionate about helping people, bringing dogs and their owners closer together, and generally improving the welfare of dogs in your community with your amazing services.

The uncomfortable truth which most failing pet business owners ignore is that the best way to make a bigger impact with your services, so you can help more dogs and their owners, is to get better at marketing.

The business who delivers an amazing service *and* presents that service better than anyone else usually ends up on top.

Mastering how to effectively market your services will enable you to build a kick-ass profitable pet business that attracts the best high-fee-paying clients, touches more people and has a bigger influence in your community.

My 'plan' is for this book to reach out and resonate with the small number of truly ambitious dog walkers, trainers, groomers and doggy daycare owners, and those just about to start a pet business (or who are just *thinking* about starting a pet business). And anyone else in this amazing industry who is already offering life-changing services, but who lacks the marketing skills to successfully promote their services and are sick of working long hours with little or no reward.

I'll be sharing my proven marketing methods that will help you claim your place at the top of the mountain and be recognised as the premier pet professional in your town, country or even the world …

However, as important as planning is, you shouldn't plan so much that you forget to take action.

As the great Napoleon Hill said, *"Plan your work, and work your plan!"*

"I'm working on my business plan" should be something you say <u>once</u>, then take action until it's done.

Actions speak louder than words

Have you heard the following statement from a friend or relative?

"This year I'm going to … lose weight, run a marathon, write a book, take a once-in-a-lifetime holiday", or any other activity you can imagine.

Usually, their *plans* involve simply *talking* about an activity. Rarely, if ever, do they transfer to the *action* phase required to actually achieve anything.

There's knowing what you *need* to do to achieve success, and then there's actually getting off your ass and fucking doing something about it.

If you are a dreamer, a thinker, a procrastinator and an 'avoider', then please return this book and I'll happily send you a refund.

This book is for the 'doers' who aren't 100% sure how to do something but will have a go anyway.

Prepare to be astonished

You'll find a lot of the ideas I'm going to share with you will be new, different, unorthodox and may even fill you with fear …

That's because they will force you to step outside of your comfort zone and develop into a new kind of business owner.

Rest assured though, *The Ultimate Pet Business Plan* is a proven, practical plan of action that will hold your hand

and walk you through the three phases of your pet business growth.

The phases are launching and establishing your new business, systemising and scaling and expanding, innovating and reinventing and dominating.

Who is this book for?

It's for any service-based sector in the pet industry.

I primarily coach dog walkers, trainers and groomers, but I've also given business-changing advice to doggy daycare owners, pet photographers, field owners and even pet pregnancy scanners. When you understand, as I do, how proper marketing works, and practise it, then you can apply effective marketing principles to any pet business.

If you've bought this book I assume you're thinking of starting a pet business, have just started one, or you have an established business you wish to expand and scale (but don't know how).

I'll be sharing with you how to best position and market your business so you can make the biggest impact possible. If you've already created a great pet business, and now you've hit a bit of a wall with your growth and are out of ideas, then I will give you some options of you how you can innovate and expand in a new direction, and if you wish, even re-invent your business entirely.

So, what makes me so qualified to teach you how to market your pet business? Well, I'm not some jumped-up guru who has done an MBA in general marketing, and who has then jumped in the pet business sector because it looks like a 'hot market'. Nor am I a dog walker who has built a business by charging low prices, who now has 3,000 Twitter followers, a Facebook group with 2,000 members, and thinks that qualifies me to teach other pet business owners about business.

So, who the hell am I? Good question, let's get to know each other a bit.

I'm Dom Hodgson, father of two boys, Alex (23) and Toby (15), husband of Beth (a schoolteacher who wouldn't let me share her age, quite right too.) I own two dogs, a cocker spaniel called Sid and a Dogue de Bordeaux called Derek, and six chickens (my favourite chicken, Sharon, passed away while I was finishing this book, more on my chickens later). Most importantly I've run my own multifaceted pet business since 2011.

My pet business journey

I started out as a dog runner then I pioneered the introduction of dog adventures. In 2012 I became a dog trainer then I ran an online dog store. I've since written three dog training books and two pet business books, and created dozens of online courses, and I've also hosted two dog podcasts.

I've built a reputation that has enabled me to speak in front of hundreds of pet business owners at seminars all over the UK. Since 2017 I've run intensive marketing bootcamps for pet business owners, and in 2019 I created the first pet business super-conference, aka IMPACT. For the last three years I've primarily mentored other pet business owners, to help them grow their business faster than their competition.

I'm not telling you any of this to brag (honest!), but rather to show you that over the last eight years I've tried lots of different things in my business.

Not all of my ventures have been successful, and I'll be sharing my low points with you too.

But I've enjoyed every step along the way, my businesses have *always* been profitable and over the last eight years I've gradually created my own dream business that enables me to write, teach, mentor and work with amazing business owners.

It's likely your dream pet business will be a lot different to mine. That's how it should be; you shouldn't want to copy me *or* anyone else.

You might no more want to write a book, or stand on stage and speak to an audience, than I want to learn how to groom or massage a dog.

What you can and definitely *should* do is 'model' your business on the success principles I lay out in this book.

See, much like the principles of dog training, the principles of successful marketing never change.

So, it doesn't matter whether you want to dominate your town with your dog walking business, have dreams to become the number-one puppy trainer, own a string of successful canine styling salons, create the world's largest doggy daycare company, or become a successful speaker, author and influencer within the industry. The marketing principles that will get you there are the same across all sectors of the pet service industry.

How to use this book

This is a short book which I've split into three parts:

1. The launch and growth of a new pet business
2. Systemising, staffing and scaling your pet business
3. Expanding, innovating and re-inventing an established pet business

Sounds like a lot to cover in one short book, right?

Not really.

At each stage of your business journey there are surprisingly few 'fundamentals' you need to master to achieve success.

I'll be sharing the 'vital few' key business principles you must get right as you hit each stage of your pet business journey. In fact, you'll be learning just seven of Dom's Golden Rules. Follow these rules and success will be yours.

You can, if you wish, skip ahead to the part which most applies to you, but I would rather you read the whole book in order, at least once (and it would be better for you to do this). That way you'll see how the principles in each phase affect the next stage of your business growth.

As an example, if you are now full and have no space to take on new clients, you will likely feel like phase two is where you need to begin, but you'd be wrong. That's because before you take on staff, or even think about taking on a staff member, you should first make your business more profitable, by increasing your prices, and pricing is a topic in phase one in the next chapter.

So, as tempting as it is to skip forward, don't do it, or, if you do, then be sure go back and re-read the whole book.

But my business is different!

Wrong, mon ami! Don't think just because you are a dog trainer, a marketing example I give for groomers doesn't apply to you, or that a promotional tip for dog walkers has no relevance to your doggy daycare business. It *does*.

Marketing is marketing is marketing, and by cross-referencing the ideas I share you'll come up with unique ways to make your business stand out from the competition. It will also give you some ideas for how you can collaborate with other pet businesses in your town.

Treat this book like a manual. Underline and highlight lightbulb moments that leap out at you.

Why does this book matter to you?

Believe it or not, by just buying this book you've probably invested more money in your marketing education than most pet professionals invest in an entire lifetime.

Marketing and promotion seem to be dirty words for the fluffy-bunny pet business owners who have a giant stick up their ass when it comes to making money from their business. That's because most of the 'average' pet business owners fall into the CPD (continuing professional development) trap of thinking they need to get better and better at 'the service' they provide.

Which is why 90% of the pet professionals out there have a hobby business which does nothing but pay for their 'seminar junkie' habit. If that sounds like you, then you are happy to remain time- and cash-poor as your business does nothing but help swell the coffers of the dog training associations who are happy to take your money.

You'll see the same old faces there and you'll tell each other the same old stories about how difficult your business is, how shitty your clients are and how empty your bank account is …

That's what average pet business owners do.

The key words there being 'average' and 'business owners'.

In order to make money from your pet business, you need to treat it like a business. You need to be good at what you do for sure, and you should passionately care about the welfare of dogs, but I'm guessing you already tick those boxes.

For you, a profitable, proven pet business and marketing plan is what's needed.

Don't underestimate how important the marketing side of your business is.

You can attend a few courses and call yourself a dog walker, a dog groomer or a dog trainer, but you'll only have a proper dog training, walking or grooming business that makes a profit with an effective marketing strategy.

I know lots of smart but stressed-out, talented but time-poor, and skilful but skint pet business owners who have failed to grasp the importance of marketing, or they lack the discipline required to successfully promote their business.

Don't become one of the pissed-off pet professionals who foolishly fall under the counterfeit charms of fake social media 'gurus', whose marketing advice consists of posting more and more updates on the ever-growing list of social media channels.

Facebook and Insta and Twitter, oh my!

Ask most pet business owners where they get their new clients from, and the answer will inevitably be 'word of mouth' and 'social media'.

"I couldn't run my business without social media."

"Of course not," I reply, *"because the concept of business didn't exist before 2004 ..."*

Social media has its place, but it's just one of the 'online' tools you need to master, in addition to the 'offline' strategies that are generally far more effective and enjoyable ways for you to grow your business, and I'll be sharing the best of them with you in this book.

So, where do we start?

Well, as Maria von Trapp used to sing, *"We start at the very beginning, a very good place to start"*, and when you turn the page we'll begin with phase one of launching and growing a pet business.

The fundamentals you learn in the next chapter will prevent you building your pet business on a house of sand and give you the strong foundations you need for lasting success.

Remember, you can get immediate access to the full audio version of this book by going to **www.growyourpetbusinessfast.com/resources**

Chapter 1

THE ULTIMATE PET BUSINESS PLAN

How to Use Your Personal Pet Business Roadmap

I was inspired to write this book as I travelled back from delivering a Grow Your Pet Business FAST seminar in South Harting in Hampshire.

That's a long drive back to sunny Sunderland in the frozen North of England (six hours since you asked).

As I steadily crawled home on the motorway, I was replaying some of the conversations I'd had with pet business owners the previous day.

All of the attendees went home with a spring in their step, and a plan for action to grow their pet business further, but while each business was in the 'pet industry' they all faced their own unique challenges.

Some were just starting out, or thinking about starting and consequently had no previous experience of running a business. This lot were enthusiastic, a little afraid and very confused about how to turn their ideas into a business.

Others had been trading for a few years or more and had a steady client base they were trying to grow further, but they were finding it a real challenge to hire reliable staff and relinquish control of 'their baby'. Consequently, they were stuck in a time-for-money swap running a business that was making money, albeit not enough, and their business was completely dependent on them being there all the time.

Then you had the more experienced pet business owners. Some of these had built a great reputation and client base, but they found they had been cruising for a few years and so gone a bit stale. They wanted a new challenge within the industry which would excite them, but they were afraid to let go of what they had built and pursue a different direction.

There's a common theme within each phase of growth.

That theme is 'fear'.

Do you remember Doctor Dolittle, who could talk to the animals? One of his most famous was the Pushmi-Pullyu, a llama with two heads and no tail.

The Pushmi-Pullyu is a good metaphor for the fear you live with as a pet business owner. Fear that can inspire you to move forward *and* hold you back in equal measure.

Fear exists at every stage of your pet business journey.

New business owners fear leaving well-paid employment and striking out on their own. Then they fear getting enough clients to pay the bills.

This fear usually drives them to offer competitive (aka cut-price) services, and they conform to what is *already* being offered in the marketplace. So, a newbie will look around at what all the existing dog walking/training/grooming businesses are offering and think *"I would like to charge more but I can't because no-one else is* **and** *I don't have the experience."*

Their fear tricks them into offering low-price services, and before they know it they are just another average pet business, working long hours for little return. If you are that 'newbie', then this chapter will show you how to *avoid* that happening.

Then you have more established businesses who have done the hard work and survived the first tough year. They now have repeat clients, which every successful business needs to survive, but they also have relationships with those clients and so they fear putting up prices.

As their reputation builds, and word of mouth kicks in, they start getting more enquiries, and pretty soon, after a year or two, they reach a tipping point and eventually get so busy they encounter the same problem that Mary and Joseph had on Christmas Eve: there's no room at the inn! Or in their case, there's no room in the van, *or* hours left in the day.

One solution is to expand your capacity and take on staff. But, that means letting go of responsibility and trusting your staff with your clients' precious dogs. You *don't* like that idea, your clients certainly *won't* like that idea and so your fear of growing the business causes you struggle on, until you finally bite the bullet and hire someone. By then you are so stressed out and busy that you do a botch job and fail to properly train your staff.

This fear of letting go stops you growing the way you want to. Don't worry though; I've got the solution to this 'staffing problem' in chapter 4.

Finally, we have the business owner who has been trading for a number of years. They've usually built a great reputation but they've often failed to turn that respectability into the 'rank one' position they deserve.

They find young upstart business owners are stealing their clients. This is usually because, through complacency or busyness, they have stopped doing the marketing they once did.

On top of that, they are becoming at best a little stale and at worst completely pissed with the business they have built. The areas of the business that once excited them and forced them to jump out of bed on a morning now *don't* have the same pull. They desire change and a new challenge, but they are so stuck in the day-to-day running of the business, that by the time they've finished their day's work they can't be bothered to make any plans. They've got the Spanish builder's problem.
'Ma ñ ana, ma ñ ana, I'll do it tomorrow' . Only tomorrow never comes.

If this is you, then chapter 4 holds the key to your particular dilemma.

Let's start with phase number one: how do you launch and grow a successful and profitable pet business?

Well, it's actually done in a very similar way to how you launch any other kind of business. You first look at the market and decide if there is any demand for the service you want to offer. Then, you look at what the competition are currently offering, and you find a way to differentiate your offering from theirs, so you stand out like a dog fart in a lift. A sweet-smelling dog fart, obviously …

Start with the market

This sounds like a very obvious business strategy, but you'd be surprised how many people start a business simply because they have a passion for 'the thing' they do, but they fail to research if anyone in their town is actually interested in buying their services.

So, let's deal with a business basic you cannot avoid. Simply offering a great service and being passionate about dogs will not guarantee you success.

In fact, passion on its own is worth about the same as a bucket of spit.

This why you see loads of new pubs, cafés, knitting shops, wedding dress makers and all kinds of pet businesses opening up in your town, only to close down again within six months.

Without a viable market you will struggle to turn your passion into profits.

Is there a demand for dog services?

You are lucky because the pet industry is a little different. If you live in the Western world there will be a huge percentage of the population in your town who own a dog. Up to 40%. This means there will be a massive demand for almost any dog-related services.

However, this also means there will be lots of other people offering the same kind of service you are thinking about offering.

I'm talking about, *cue dramatic music*, dun, dun duuuuuun!

The competition

You can rest assured, no matter what pet business you are starting, there will be LOTS of other pet businesses in your town already competing for the clients you want. And if you are lucky enough to live somewhere that hasn't been saturated yet, then don't get too cocky because as soon as they see you making money with your pet service, someone will try to copy you.

This is simply how business works.

Coca-Cola has Pepsi challenging them for fridge space.

McDonald's has Burger King trying to take a bite out of their market share.

Even the mighty Amazon fears the competition.

So, how do you create a pet business that is different and better than anything anyone else can offer either now, or in the future?

You do that by following the Seven Golden Rules I will share with you in this book. But, before we dive into those, let me tell you how my business journey began and how I dealt with the competition.

Dom's dog walking story …

When I started my business eight years ago there were a lot fewer dog walkers around than there are today, but there was still some competition.

This was my first business. I did bring some marketing experience from my previous sales job, so I knew I needed to have some kind of USP (unique selling proposition) which made my new business stand out.

Your USP is the thing that differentiates you from the competition. This is a key factor that will determine how successful your business is in the future.

I looked at the competition and wasn't too impressed with what I saw. Everyone was offering 30-minute or one-hour 'walks'. I looked at the market and saw that people were moving away from getting a traditional 'Heinz 57 mongrel' and instead buying or adopting pedigree dogs, especially high-energy working and gun dogs.

What I did might sound really obvious now, but you'd be surprised how many people start a pet business and simply look at what the competition are doing then copy their services almost exactly. They clone their competitors' prices and services, then they struggle to figure out why their business doesn't stand out.

The answer is to look for a gap in the market that your specialised service can fill. I'm talking about having a 'niche' offering which instantly makes you look like a specialist, instead of a generalist.

As part of my research into the market I noticed a lot of people owned working and pedigree dogs these days, but because they worked or just didn't have time, they weren't able to give their 'high energy' dogs the exercise and stimulation they needed.

I had immediately a target breed for my services – working and hunting dogs.

Action point – Take some time to research what your local dog population looks like in your town. These are the people who will be your customers and clients. Are there already lots of dog walkers, trainers, groomers or doggy daycares in your town? Then you will need to think very carefully about how you are going to make your service 'stand out' from the more established businesses. The more creative you are, the easier it will be to get your message out there.

Here's a few examples. Are you located slap bang in the middle of a city centre where there are lots of frustrated and yappy chihuahuas and pugs? Then maybe it's worth niching as a small-dog specialist whose service turns handbag yappers into backpack adventure hounds.

Are you a dog trainer in a city centre who sees lots of off-leash and out-of-control working breeds? You could position yourself as the dog employment officer whose mission is to give a job and a purpose to all the bored and destructive 'dogs on the dole'.

Generally, the bigger the city you live in, the more crucial it is that you niche down and carve a slice off the market which you can claim as your own.

How to make your business different to the competition

Next up I looked at what dog walkers were offering in my town, across the UK and the USA, and I came up with a new service which hadn't been offered in my town. Everyone else was offering a standard 30-minute or 60-minute walk at the time, so I chose to offer an enhanced exercise service with a 1.5-hour 'dog adventure'.

I started by offering dog running services, but they didn't catch on. I think if I'd been based in LA then it might have been more popular, but the people of Sunderland weren't ready for that, yet ... This turned out to be a blessing in disguise, though, as I quickly switched away from running, and 'adventures' became my specialised service.

So, Pack Leader Dog Adventures was born. I had a stand-out service which was different to anything else my competitors offered, and my marketing message was perfectly matched to the market I was targeting.

My target market was wealthier pedigree dog owners who loved their dogs dearly, but because of work, business or other commitments were unable to give the dogs the exercise and stimulation they needed. The people I was targeting didn't necessarily need to be millionaires with helicopters and mansions, although it would be sensible for you to target those as well. What you are really after is the small number of dog owners in your town who are prepared to invest in the very best products and services.

And being premium is Dom's Golden Rule Number 1, so turn the page and let's deep-dive into phase one of *The Ultimate Pet Business Plan*...

Chapter 2

The Ultimate Pet Business Plan

Phase One – How to Launch and Grow Your Profitable Pet Business

Before I started my pet business, I worked as sales rep for Imperial Tobacco. I did this for 10 years and learned a lot about marketing, features and benefits, relationship selling, and how brands grow.

Not being a smoker myself I was surprised at the differing price of the cigarettes. You had your expensive brands that were perceived to be cool or in some way a luxury. Then there were the middle-of-the-road brands which were usually the most popular; then you had the cheap and cheerful brands at the bottom that usually had a special or reduced price sticker on them and were always the choice of the bargain-hunting customer.

It won't surprise you to learn that the company used to make a lot more money from the premium brands than they did from the middle-of-the-road varieties and way more than the cheap brands. However, a huge surprise to me was that the stuff inside the cigarettes was almost exactly the same in the cheaper brands as it was in the most expensive variety.

That meant the intrinsic value for the customer, and the much higher profits earned by the company came from how the premium brands were packaged up, promoted, presented and perceived by the customer.

Then I looked around and I realised that every industry selling products and services could be categorised into a top, middle and bottom entry.

The cheapest café in my town sold their grub at the lowest prices to the customers who could only afford that offering.

In contrast, the Michelin-starred restaurant (and yes, we do have at least one of those, even in Sunderland) could charge outrageously higher prices for a meal that contained higher-quality ingredients, was presented more stylishly, but provided less actual food on a plate.

And the high-end restaurant obviously attracts high-end clients who desire the best food and experience, and are prepared to pay top dollar prices to get what they want.

You'll find the same thing happens in every industry in every town all over the world.

Even yours, dear reader.

Take a drive or a walk around the town you live and you'll find there's a top, middle and a bottom provider for every service from hairdressers to lawyers, cafés to funeral parlours. And if you look hard enough you'll also find a luxury and a bargain basement offering too.

In fact, you won't even need to drive. Just look out of your window and you'll see people driving beaten-up death-trap cars and vans, and you'll also see Land Rovers, Ferraris and all kinds of pimped-up transportation.

So, if there is a top, middle and bottom offering for every service, why can't there be a top, middle and bottom in the pet industry?

There can, and there is!

You just need to step up and claim your place at the premium end of the table. This brings us to the first of Dom's Golden Rules for success.

Golden Rule Number 1 – Be Premium

The great thing about running your own business is you get to choose who to sell to and at what price you want to sell your services. So, if you have that choice, why wouldn't you want to charge premium prices to the best customers?

This is *exactly* what I did when I started my adventure business. Everyone else was charging £10 an hour for dog walks (tragically, some dog walkers are *still* charging those prices) whereas I doubled that price, from the beginning. I offered a more comprehensive service for sure, but I didn't spend twice as long with the dogs to earn twice the money of my competitors.

Instead, just like the Michelin-starred restaurant, I packaged up my offering so it was more appealing (and suitable) for dog owners in my town who wanted an extra-special service for their dogs.

Charging higher prices meant I could offer a better service than my competitors, and I attracted the best dog owners to my business.

"But I don't feel like I can justify selling my service for a higher price. I'm not different enough, and I don't have enough experience."

Bollocks you don't!

Experience is overrated. You need to be good at what you do, but it's not difficult to achieve that. You'll find that most of your competition who've been around a long time aren't *that* good either.

They don't have 10 years of innovation behind them, but rather 10 years of doing the same thing, the same way, every single day of their career.

Be Premium Client Case Study – Tim's Premium Upsell Story …

"When I started by pet business, I spent countless hours researching other companies and looking at the services they offered, and I matched their prices. In some cases, I even offered lower prices so I could be the cheapest around.

I never had the confidence to charge more and was worried that this would lose me a lot of clients that I had worked so hard to gain. For many years I continued down this same path, and granted, I got clients, but due to the lower prices I was charging it resulted in 10 times the work for very little return.

My business offers a number of services, and I have always been more than aware of the potential and return the business could offer, but I never had the balls to do anything about it and risk losing everything (or so I thought!), and in all honesty I didn't really have the marketing knowledge to implement any changes.

I was recommended Dom by a friend who is also a client of Dom's, and I spent a few months doing my homework and research on him.

I eventually invested in Dom and became a Diamond member (best thing I ever did). Since becoming a Diamond member Dom has made me realise what I am worth and what the business is worth. During my time as a Diamond member, we have had numerous discussions about how I can make my business a premium business.

Following Dom's advice, I implemented Dom's Golden Rules Numbers 1 and 2, increased my prices for all of our services and also introduced a new service as part of our daycare service. Our doggy adventure daycare was something that no other doggy daycares in the area offered, but Dom convinced me to go straight in with a premium price.

I expected to lose a few clients to the price increase, but I was totally wrong. I lost one client due to the price, and the rest are still using the services but now paying premium prices, which is great for the business and great for my bank account. Following Dom's advice has proven that people are willing to pay premium prices, and a simple increase in price has massively increased my yearly turnover.

Offering premium prices means I now have more to invest back into the business, more to spend on my family and I'm not worrying from month to month about needing to pay the bills. In the first month of increasing the prices, the business made an additional £800, which goes to prove this shit works!"

Tim Jackson
www.pets2impress.com

However, not being different from the competition will make it harder for your business to stand out so you can justify your higher prices. That's where Dom's next Golden Rule comes in.

And that is **Dom's Golden Rule Number 2 – Be Specialised**.

Nailing it with a niche

Don't fall into the trap of thinking you need to be more qualified or more experienced than your competitors to make money in your business. You don't.

You need to be good, of course, but you won't rise to the top by *just* being better.

You need to be better *and* different to your competition. Being better isn't enough. What happens when someone starts offering your service who is better than you are?

When you are 'different', you are able to communicate your specific marketing message to a certain section of the market.

Most businesses, especially new businesses, resist 'niching down', but those that have the balls (or the ladyballs) to do it usually make the most money.

What can your speciality be?

You could be a puppy specialist dog trainer, who offers mainly puppy-related services. Or a squashy-faced dog walker (I don't mean an ugly dog walker; I mean a walker who only walks flat-faced breeds …) You could be a shih-tzu-only stylist who only grooms shih-tzus. You could have a doggy daycare that only admits older dogs. You could be a photographer who specialises in gundog portraits. Think about what you are good at and where your passion lies.

Niching with your industry also makes your marketing so much easier, because everything you do to promote your business will be related to your niche.

This makes you stand out because while your competition are marketing to 'dog owners' in general, you'll be marketing to a small segment of the market that represent the specific niche you have claimed.

Be Specialised Client Case Study – Harriet's Gundog Story...

"Pawtastic has been running for about five years. I have always wanted to stand out from all the other dog walkers and wanted to make more money. About a year ago, after following Dom's advice from his other book *Walk Yourself Wealthy* be more specialised. I decided to niche down in my business.

I love gundogs; my parents had a labrador. Most of my clients' dogs were labradors and, added bonus, I loved walking them.

So I decided to niche to gundogs and went the whole hog. I rebranded my business. Pawtastic Gundog Adventures was born, and I have a new 'gundog'-focused website.

As Dom says in his latest book, you position yourself as the natural choice for people who own dogs in that niche, and it did just that. I can charge more and marketing is a lot easier. I talk about gundogs in every piece of marketing material. It took a lot of ladyballs to do it, but it has been a real game changer for me!"

Harriet Goodall
www.pawtasticgundogadventures.co.uk

Why niching matters

If you've ever gone underground into a train station in a big city, you'll have passed by the row of posters on the wall as you descend on the escalator. Somehow, you manage to ignore and forget almost all of them, except the one that is advertising something that interests you.

It doesn't matter how busy or distracted you are, your eyes magnetically lock onto that one poster straight away, and you might even turn around and crane your neck to finish reading it before the escalator takes it out of view. And if you didn't finish reading it, then you'll be looking out for it on the return leg, and ignoring all the others.

Why do we do this?

Because we are only interested in information that is relevant to us.

We only care about stuff we are interested in.

And when you niche down, you can promote your pet business in a similar way.

All dogs are wonderful, but in the eyes of their owners, certain breeds rank more highly than others.

You and I are no different.

I bet you've got a breed, or a type of dog, that you prefer over all others.

For me and my family it's the Dogue de Bordeaux. We own a DDB, and Derek is our second DDB rescue.

If my Dogue had to have an operation, and I had the choice between someone who is a chihuahua or a mastiff specialist, which one do you think I would choose?

Exactly!

Now, let's say you were thinking of starting a doggy day-care and when you did the research I suggested earlier, you discovered there were a lot of bulldogs and French bull-dogs in your town, so you were leaning towards offering a daycare service that would purely cater for brachycephalic breeds.

You call it the Squashyfaced Academy.

Well, whenever a bulldog, French bulldog or pug owner is looking for a daycare service, their eyes are going to be drawn to your business in a similar way your eyes are drawn to the poster on the escalator wall that is relevant to you. They are going to ignore all the other daycare owners and be grateful they found you.

How to be a big fish!

Being a specialist instead of a generalist means you become a big fish in a small pond, and you position yourself as the natural choice for people who own dogs in that niche.

There will be a higher perception of authority among the dog owners you are targeting, which means you can charge higher prices.

This is why specialist surgeons earn more than doctors who are general practitioners. The surgeons aren't necessarily smarter or more skilled overall, but they have concentrated their efforts into becoming an expert in a few particular disciplines, or even one. This means they can charge higher prices, which also means they need *fewer* clients to make a fantastic amount of money.

You can do the same thing when you specialise in your pet business.

In short, if you want to earn more, work less, stand out and make your business easier to find by people who you really want to work with, then you need to niche down.

So, first step is to get your thinking cap on and decide how you can start your business out on the best footing by carving out a niche for yourself, from day one.

This advice also applies to more established business owners who already have a healthy business. In many ways it's easier for established businesses to niche because you simply look at your list of current customers and see what breed, or problem behaviour, makes up the largest percentage of your client base.

Don't worry too much about your competition copying you. It happens now and again, and to a degree you can protect your business name with a trademark, but the chances are most of your competition won't have the wit or the courage to copy your specialised services.

Once you've got your marketing message nailed, then you need to figure out a way to promote your services to the correct dog owners in your town.

As P.T. Barnum said , *"Without promotion something terrible happens. Nothing."*

There's nothing more depressing than meeting a passionate pet business owner who offers a life-changing service but who doesn't have any customers.

So, how do you go about putting the word 'out there', so you can build awareness about your business, and get some paying clients on the books?

This is where a lot of pet professionals fail miserably.

They have no effective means of finding the dog owners they are trying to help, and they inevitably rely on social media to advertise their services.

Unfortunately, doing 'free engagement' type self-promotion on social media isn't the best (or even the second, third or fourth best) way to market your pet business.

The social media myth

These days social media is considered to be the silver bullet which you must have in your 'marketing gun', but which bullet should you be firing? Facebook, Instagram, Pinterest, Twitter? Blogs, YouTube, Tumblr, Messenger and the list goes on …

The fact is most social media platforms will be a complete waste of time for you because none of your potential customers will be even using that media.

Facebook seems to be the default platform for most pet business owners, but it's very difficult to get clients using only Facebook, certainly high-fee-paying, affluent clients.

The times they are a-changing …

Once upon a time it was easier to market yourself on Facebook, but now, with a third of the world's population regularly using it, it's more difficult than ever to get your unique marketing message in front of your target client on Facebook.

That is unless you are using paid, targeted adverts, which can work very well, ***if*** you know what you are doing. Unless you've got deep pockets and an in-depth understanding of the advertising platform, then I would steer clear of FB adverts, especially boosted posts, which do nothing but 'boost' Facebook profits with your hard-earned cash.

So, if social media isn't all it's cracked up to be, then why do I still use it?

Great question, and the answer is I use as many offline and online marketing methods as I can that I know work for me.

So I run Facebook adverts and do the occasional LIVE post. I also write blogs and have a YouTube channel. I write a daily email to my list, and I also have a weekly podcast, **The Poodle to Pitbull Pet Business Podcast**.

But, I also do a LOT of offline marketing.

I send a monthly paper-and-ink newsletter to people who request it, or who have bought from me in the past. I'm regularly featured in newspapers and magazines, and I regularly do in-person events all around the UK, and I host a couple of big events of my own every year.

However, I now run a worldwide pet business marketing and mentoring company, so I *should* be promoting myself across all effective mediums.

But you don't need to, and you *shouldn't*. Phew!

No, what you need is a 'local' marketing medium that will quickly get 'eyes' on your new pet business, and to do that I would recommend you get off your butt (and off social media) and go fishing!

Fish where the fishes are

I feel lucky in that when I started my business there wasn't as much excitement about social media as there is these days (Facebook has been available in the UK since 2006, but it was still wasn't being widely used in 2011 when I started).

This meant I had to do other things to get my name out there and get some clients.

So, what did I do?

PR – I got some local press coverage, which helped get my business name out there. This was made easier because my adventure business was different to all the other dog 'walkers' out there. This is another reason for you to specialise. Trust me, you'll find it easier to get press coverage if you are 'King of the Cockers', 'The Terrible Terrier Trainer' or you run 'the Big Dog Bath Palace' than if you are just seen as another 'average' pet business owner with no personality or story.

I've since made PR and 'getting my mush in the paper' a much more prominent and consistent marketing activity, and I'll go more into this in a later chapter, but for now, just know that you should take any opportunity you can to get your face, name and services advertised for free on local media outlets.

Networking – I joined some local networking groups, and although I didn't get many new clients from this, it did teach me how to present and promote my business in a way that got people's attention.

Host/parasite (or co-operative) marketing – This was a game-changer for me, and I suspect it will be for you too. I got some leaflets printed, and I spent a weekend handing them out to dog owners in a large local pet store. That one activity made me more money (over £150,000 over the next six years) than anything else I've done before or since. This is where I recommend you start too.

Social media or local marketing?

See, when you think about it rationally, is it more sensible to try to filter out the dog owners in your town who might be interested in your services from the two billion people on Facebook, OR go directly to the other pet business in your town (who aren't direct competitors of yours) who are already selling to dog owners who would also make great clients for you?

I hope you can see it's the latter option which will be way more beneficial.

People buy people

When they hire you to train, groom or walk their dog, people in your town aren't just buying the service. They are buying YOU.

They want to know they can trust you to take great care of their dog, and the best way to communicate you are a trustworthy and knowledgeable pet professional is to get out there and start selling and promoting your services directly to the people who will buy them. And you do that with your own media.

Golden Rule Number 3 – Create Your Own Media

Now, don't worry. I'm not suggesting you buy an advert on a local TV channel, or hire a billboard that sits on the main route into your town.

What I'm suggesting is an easier, cheaper and more effective method …

You are going to create your own newsletter.

Your newsletter is the best way to communicate your marketing message and convince dog owners in your town to give you a call.

Why a newsletter?

There are lots of reasons why a newsletter works, and I go into more detail about this in the free training you can access with this book. But these three reasons will do for now.

Newsletters get read. Newsletters are a bit like newspapers, which means newsletters get read. They really do. We are conditioned to read newsletters and newspapers from an early age. Think about newsletters you received from your school or church (if you attended). They sent a regular newsletter as a way of keeping in touch and communicating 'news'.

Newsletters get kept. Texts get read, emails get ignored and FB statuses and tweets are forgotten in the blink of an eye. But your paper-and-ink newsletter will get picked up, kept and eventually read. It'll get read and enjoyed quicker if you put some interesting stories in there.

Newsletters are interesting and newsletters *aren't* leaflets. How many leaflets come through your door in an average week? Ten, 20, more? Now, how many of those do you actually read? Exactly, none. Leaflets get binned, almost *immediately*, because they scream *'I'm Selling Something. BUY MY SHIT!'* Your newsletter, however, if you keep it light, interesting, relevant, local and 'newsy', will be read and enjoyed by whoever picks it up.

How to produce your newsletter

It doesn't need to be anything fancy.

Just a simple A4 size, four-page newsletter in which you'll tell your story, communicate your USP and reassure the reader of your skills by including testimonials, client stories and case studies.

I like to include a fun story about something interesting that happened to me that month. Also, there is a testimonial or 'dog of the month' section, a piece about something local to my town, like a favourite or secret dog walk and something light about me and my family that shows the reader I'm a real person. The thing about a newsletter is you don't talk about dogs all the time … put your personality into it and you'll better communicate your values and attract your ideal client.

How to distribute your newsletter

A big part of the 'local marketing' strategy is about aligning yourself with other pet business who complement yours. So, dog walkers, trainers and groomers should be connecting with vets, doggy diners and pet shops. Ultimately, you can share your clients with non-competing pet businesses in your town, and your newsletter will be the perfect introduction to those new clients.

Create Your Own Media Client Case Study – Carrie's Newsletter Story…

"So I don't really like Facebook. Yeah, I said it out loud, but I still can't break away fully from it; there is an addiction there that I cannot fully break. I have cut my daily use down to one hour per day for the past year and try to be strict as I can with that. I don't think it's healthy to be on there, and it really is a time waste, hours and hours of your life wasted, scrolling away. Seriously, I have better things to do with my time, but every now again I do catch myself doing it.

But, I hear you say, I need it to promote my business! Nope, you really don't, not unless you have plenty of money to spend on an expert to do Facebook adverts for you. I have wasted a lot of money 'boosting' my posts when I thought I knew what I was doing, targeting who saw it, using the filters – or so I thought, but I have been proved wrong. One of the reasons I've not come away from it completely is I do use it for work, but not in a way many others do. I post up pictures for my clients to see their dogs and cats on the internet. I will use it to put up events and try to promote them in groups. But really, if I am honest, it is not where my clients come from. Yes, I may get a few from there, but the bulk of my clients come from elsewhere – the clients I now aim at aren't on the local groups as they aren't looking for the cheapest walker. They want someone who gets their dog.

I don't even reply to Messenger requests on my page. I ask them to email me with their enquiry. What many others see as marketing on Facebook, I see as wasting time – posting up memes, trying to promote classes, etc. – as I now know such a small percentage of people actually see them. I was told only 1 in 100 actually see the post. That post that took you 30 minutes to write and put together less than 10 people may have seen it. Time wasted, and as a small business owner, time isn't something I want to waste. I want to make the most of it.

So, I don't use Facebook anymore – yes, I used to try to use it to fill classes, but it didn't really work. My puppy class is now always full and has a waiting list; I promote it through various forms of offline marketing – sending physical post, whether that be a postcard sent in the post, or a newsletter, or having a stand at an event and speaking to people. People pick up my newsletter in shops and contact me for training or to get booked onto my adventures. If I had stuck to doing what everyone else was doing on Facebook, I wouldn't be in the place I am now, looking to hire my third assistant. My newsletters get people's attention, and I enjoy making them."

Carrie Stuthridge
www.carriescanines.co.uk

Newsletter bonus

I practise what I preach and produce a free four-page monthly newsletter, 'The Pack Leader Business Gazette', for everyone who buys a copy of this book. In it, I tell stories and give business hints and tips, which helps me keep in touch with my tribe. To sign up for my free paper-and-ink newsletter, go to **www.growyourpetbusinessfast.com** and click the free resources tab.

Summary

That concludes phase one of launching and growing a profitable pet business. I've shared the first three Golden Rules that will unlock and unleash your premium, niched pet business into the world, and give you a unique communication method (your newsletter) that tells people you exist and gets eyes on your business.

Let's recap the first three Golden Rules.

Golden Rule Number 1 – Be Premium. Being premium from day one is the main reason I have been able to achieve so much in my business. Cash flow has always been good, and my higher prices mean I have always attracted the best clients and avoided the stressful bottom feeders who drain your energy and keep you skint. Someone is going to be the cheapest pet business and someone is going to be the most expensive. Which one would you rather be?

Golden Rule Number 2 – Be Specialised. Many pet businesses fail because they fail to stand out, and the easy option for any new business is to copy (or do very much the same as) what the competition are currently. But if you do that you immediately camouflage your business by blending into the crowd. By following the second key to success you will ensure your business is different, and by niching down you make it easy for customers who are looking for a specialised service to find you.

Golden Rule Number 3 – Create Your Own Media. Creating a monthly (or even a quarterly) newsletter is the quickest and easiest way to get local eyes on your new business. Your newsletter will communicate your premium, specialised service to the dog owners you want to work with. You can literally put it directly in their hands, or through their letterbox. Don't be beguiled by the magical allure of social media. Targeted paper-and-ink promotional materials have worked for the last 100 years, and they will still be here in another 100, long after the current social media fads have disappeared.

Chapter 3

The Ultimate Pet Business Plan

Phase Two – How to Staff, Scale and Systemise Your Pet Business

So, you've successfully launched your pet business, and you now have a steady stream of enquiries that are bringing in excellent clients you love working with.

You have the wind in your sails, your reputation is growing and you finally paid back your credit card (or whatever you borrowed from family members) and have some money in the bank …

… but, one thing you *don't* have is any more time to service the new clients who have heard great things about you, and now want to use your training, walking, daycare or grooming services.

If that hasn't happened *yet*, then keep working through Golden Rules 1, 2 and 3, and it soon *will*.

That was certainly *my* experience.

How a premium pet business grows

Because I was premium priced from day 1, my business grew slightly slower than if I'd been charging rock-bottom prices like my competitors, but after about 18 months I was full to bursting and had little time available, and no energy in my legs, to take on any more clients.

So, when you are full and still getting enquiries, this must be the right time to take on a staff member, right?

Wrong!

Many pet professionals make the mistake of hiring staff as soon as they run out of time to serve new clients.

I know what you are thinking: that's how businesses grow, right? When demand outstrips supply, you have to increase the capacity.

Well, that's *one* way to do it. But there is a better way to ensure your business grows in a sustainable and profitable way, before you encounter the headaches and stress that come with taking on staff.

Supply and demand isn't *just* about increasing supply to meet demand. The other, often less popular but vastly more profitable, option is to **increase your prices**.

Increasing your prices will dampen demand for your services, and increase the amount of money you earn from your current clients.

Increasing your prices doesn't bring any additional advertising, administration or production costs. You simply change the digits on your website and inform your current clients by text, email, letter (or all three) that you are putting them up.

You'll be pleasantly surprised how few clients will complain, or even comment, when you increase your prices. Yes, one or two *might* quibble, but the chances are they will be the cheapskate PITA (pain in the arse) clients who are constantly complaining, and making your life a misery.

You know, the ones who expect you to be there at the drop of a hat, complain about your prices and pay you late, that's if they pay you at all.

If you currently have a few, or lots, of those clients, then that's a clear sign your prices are way too low.

Making your pet business as profitable as possible should always be priority number one, and the easiest way to increase your profits is to increase your prices. And if no-one blinks when you increase your prices, then you can do it again, and again, until you meet some resistance.

Those with eagle eyes will notice we are revisiting **Golden Rule Number 1 – Be Premium**.

So, why are we going back to the first rule?

Well, if you implemented Golden Rules 2 and 3, then you'll already run a specialised service (your niche) which positions you as an expert, and you'll have an effective medium to communicate your amazing business (your newsletter). Your niche and your newsletter help cement your premium status.

And as your reputation grows, so should your prices.

The thing about being premium is there is no upper limit to what you can charge. Not all of your clients will come with you on your business journey; that's fine. It's your choice whether you want to find clients who *will* pay your higher prices, or limit your income because you are too scared to put your prices up.

In the next chapter I'll be talking about how you position yourself as a leader and expert, which is what you need to do if you want to be able to charge outrageous prices. That's for later …

For now, please don't skip over this crucial pricing lesson as you search for the staffing and scaling secrets to come, and make sure you push the price as far as you can BEFORE you take on staff.

Business is a game of margin, not volume, and the extra profit you make will mean you can pay your staff better wages and still make a good margin for yourself.

I've seen many pet business owners become 'busy fools' who make little or no money from their business because there wasn't sufficient margin in their core service. This means they end up with a business that keeps the ever-expanding customer base happy, *and* pays the staff wages, but leaves little financial reward for the business owner.

And as much as you love dogs, you need to remember that first and foremost you are running a business.

The job of a business is to make money for the shareholders, and as the business owner you are the sole (or certainly the main) shareholder. Don't forget that.

Of course, you may decide you don't want staff at all, in which case you can keep increasing your prices until you have a small, select group of clients who pay you lots of money. These will become your 'core client base' and they won't be tempted by any of the cheaper competition that keep appearing like weeds in a flower bed.

When is the right time to take on staff?

For most business owners it makes sense at some point to at least take on part-time staff. This enables you to take some time off and still provide a service for your clients, which means you can continue to make some money when you aren't working in the business, and you keep your clients happy.

The big stumbling block for most pet business owners is not that they don't want to take on staff to help their business grow; it's that they can't face the thought of giving up control of their business.

You assume that no-one else will care as much about the clients as you do, that they won't deliver the same levels of service as you AND that the clients won't let anyone else train, walk or groom their dog.

Well, I've got good news for you. You are *wrong* about all of the above.

Actually, that's not strictly true. Your staff *won't* care as much as you do about the business; how can they? It's YOUR business, after all.

But you *can* put procedures in place to help them deliver a consistently high level of service that will placate your valued clients and convince them they are still going to receive the same fantastic service from your business, even if it isn't 'you' who is delivering that service.

I must make a confession here because when my business was around 18 months old, I also felt that I couldn't relinquish control of my services. I convinced myself that I was the only one who could do what I was doing, and this held me back from growing and scaling.

So, how did I fix that?

The same way you will fix your business, by creating a signature system.

Golden Rule Number 4 – Systemise Your Business and Create a Signature Success System

Your signature system is the step-by-step methodology for how you train, groom, walk or photograph the dogs in your care.

Your signature system defines the process by which you deliver your services. This makes you stand out from the competition (who won't have such a system), and it reassures your clients that you have a reliable, proven method for delivering your service.

Because this system details the processes for how you deliver your service, it can also be used to teach staff members how to do exactly what it is you do, the way *you* do it.

From burgers to barkers

McDonald's is probably the best example of how you can successfully scale a business by implementing brilliantly detailed systems which *don't* rely on the owner of the business to deliver them.

If you're a vegetarian, then stick with me here because there are some important business lessons you need to learn …

McDonald's started out as a single drive-in restaurant run by a pair of brothers, Dick and Mac McDonald, in southern California.

And McDonald's didn't develop into the huge success they are today (34,000 outlets in 126 countries) by making a better hamburger.

No, McDonald's' innovation was creating a better business system – they developed better methods, systems and controls – which meant they could lower costs, and sell their products cheaper to the public, which allowed them to grow and be more profitable.

A travelling salesman called Ray Kroc bought the rights to franchise this 'speedy' system, and the rest, as they say, is history.

So, what systems do you have in your own business?

Usually, when I ask that question to my coaching clients, I get told, *"I don't have a system as such; I just train the dog"*, or *"I just groom it the way I always groom that breed"*, or *"I don't use any system; I just pick the dog up and walk him"*.

If you think that, then you are severely underestimating how complex and sophisticated your current systems are.

Systemise Your Business Client Case Study – Sally's Signature System Story …

"One of my biggest stumbling blocks was being different to everyone else. I changed the walks I offered to three types of adventures, Bronze, Silver and Gold, but I still felt that they didn't make me any different.

Dom helped me see that I was offering more on my walks than most other dog walkers. This got me thinking about creating a signature system, so I put a name to my concept and got it trademarked too.

P•E•T® Play, Engage & Train came about because Dom gave me the confidence to believe that I was actually different and unique. I now have a signature system that shows I'm different, will help me to grow my business and showcase me as an expert."

Sally Cousins
www.wooferswalkies.com

Creating your signature system

To identify the system, you need to break down your regular routine into its constituent parts.

As an example, think about what the first step of your 'process' is when you meet/train/groom/walk a dog.

Let's take dog walking as an example:

- What do you do with the dogs when you walk them?
- Do you play with them? If so, what kind of games do you play?
- On average, how many times do you play each game?
- Do you take treats with you?
- How do you decide when it's safe to let the dogs off lead?
- When do you decide to put them back on lead?

We can go even further back in the process too:

- How do you decide where to walk your dogs?
- How do you decide which dogs can be walked together and which need to be walked on their own?
- How do you safely get the dog to and from the van?
- How do you make sure the owner's house is secure?

The answers to these questions will become the procedures that go in the manual which you will use to train up your staff members, so they can deliver the same high levels of service which you currently give your clients.

And that's the beautiful thing about a signature system. Almost everyone already has one; they just don't realise it, or they don't think of it as a 'system'.

You basically take the routine above and put all of the 'actions' into a logical order that is easy to follow.

Your systems should be detailed, but *don't* be overly technical with the procedures you map out.

Remember, your staff probably won't be as passionate, *or* as knowledgeable, as you, so make it easy for them to learn, and keep your procedures safe, simple to understand and easy to action.

You can begin documenting your systems with the staff member when you take them on, but ideally you should start systemising your business processes now, *before* you start hiring.

Doing it now means you can really nail down each process, and test it to make it as effective and foolproof as possible.

It can be a tedious job at times, but this is how you go from being a one-man (or woman) band, whose business can only function when you are there, to being a systemised company that can grow and scale up, while maintaining the same level of service that built your reputation.

Systemise the Business Case Study – Suzanne's Staff Handbook Story …

"When my business, Edinburgh Holistic Dogs, was a just over a year old, all my Adventure Filled Walks were more or less full, thanks to Dom and his help within the Pet Business Inner Circle.

I knew I wanted to grow by hiring a dog walker to be able to accommodate the enquiries for walks that I was turning away. Before I went through the process of hiring someone, Dom had said I should write up my system or handbook so any new hire can do the same job as me. I thought this would be easy-peasy. I mean how hard can it be to write up what I do?

Once I started typing, I realised exactly how much goes into a single dog walk. Most of what I do is now second nature to me, but I had to sit down and really think about every step that's involved in being a dog walker who offers a premium service. I had to also remember that any potential hire might not have as much knowledge as me when it comes to handling multiple dogs.

So, 35 pages later, I have my handbook; it covers everything a dog walker working for me needs to know, such as how to prepare their car/van for dogs, what equipment they should be using, how to provide the same adventures I do, and how they should present themselves to clients and the general public, and I also list any potential problems they could come across and how to handle them … plus a lot more.

Even though I have trained my staff myself, it has been invaluable to also hand over a handbook for the walker to read in their own time. It hasn't happened, but if I found the walker not performing their duties correctly, I could refer them back to the handbook.

Having my own handbook has also been a selling point to customers, as a lot of potential new clients come to me via referrals and word of mouth, so it helps to show any new client that their dog will be treated the same with my staff as they would be if I was walking them.

Granted, it took time to put together, but it has been more than worth it."

Suzanne Gould
www.edinburghholisticdogs.co.uk

In effect, systemising your business this way enables you to help more dog owners with your amazing services. And who doesn't want that?

Don't get too distracted by the 'dog walking' example either. This also applies to trainers, groomers, daycare owners, pet massage, hydrotherapists, pet scanners and even pet photographers.

You have a way of doing things that is based on what you learned from your mentors, and the experience you've had in business so far. It's the system that's already in your head; you just need to make it real and get it out of your head and into a manual.

So, that's a brief look at why you need to systemise your pet business if you want to scale, expand or even just be able to take time away from the business without it shutting down because you aren't there.

And even if you don't want the hassle of staffing your business yet, there is one thing you definitely should do, and that is implement **Golden Rule Number 5 – Sell More Stuff**.

We are returning to the golden arches once again because if you've ever reached the counter or sat in the drive-through at McDonald's (other fast food outlets are available), you'll have heard the immortal words:

"Would you like to go large?"

Or

"Would you like fries with that?"

This isn't just a *fast-food* thing. All restaurants employ the upselling technique. They get you in (and sometimes break even) with the promise of a good-value meal, but they make money on the desserts, coffee and the wine list.

Amazon are probably the ultimate example of a business that effortlessly encourages you to open your wallet so you keep on clicking and buying more stuff.

Have you ever bought a book because Amazon tells you that *"People who bought this, also bought this?"*

I know I have.

Before you know it, the one item you wanted has become a basket full of things.

And there are lots of big business lessons you can swipe from the likes of Amazon and McDonald's and implement in your small pet business.

The main takeaway is you need to sell your clients more stuff.

Don't underestimate what your clients will spend on their pooches …

For some reason (usually fear, once again) we fail to sell, or even to *offer*, our existing clients more of our services. I experienced this last year when we welcomed six little hens into our home …

Dom's chicken run story

In 2015 we upped sticks and left the town house where we'd lived for 20 years, and we moved to the outskirts of Sunderland to a village called Ryhope. This is actually near to where I grew up when I was a kid. Our new home was an old farmhouse, and as well as some dilapidated barns and lots of decorating to do, it also came with a good-sized enclosed garden.

It had been a longstanding dream to own chickens, ever since Beth and I had watched Hugh Fearnley-Whittingstall do the same thing on the first season of *River Cottage* many years ago, and now with our enclosed garden we could finally do it.

So, one day in early spring, my youngest son, Toby, and I went to the local chicken farm. We picked out four fine birds, then went into the shop and ordered a coop, some food and a few other bits and bobs.

The bill for everything was quite substantial, but I didn't care. I wanted the best of everything I could afford.

The lady who ran the joint kept us right with what we needed to buy, but she always seemed to show us the cheapest option version first. She would pick up a plastic water dispenser and say *"This one is £12, but I would recommend this better one for £14."* To which I replied *"How much is that stainless steel one behind that looks like it's just come from the* Darling Buds of May *TV set, because that's the one I want."*

It was more double the price of the cheaper plastic version, but I didn't care about that, and that's not because I'm some kind of Rockefeller who throws money around like confetti. Remember, this was my dream chicken experience. I'd looked forward to this day for years. I certainly wasn't going to scrimp on my dream.

So, I got what I wanted, but they missed out on receiving a lot more of my money, not because I said no, but because they failed to sell me more stuff.

Similarly, your clients aren't going to scrimp when it comes to providing the best groom, walk, training session, massage, daycare experience or anything else they want for *their* precious pooch. And if you offer them 'more of the same' or an 'extra-special version' of your service, a percentage of your clients will take you up on it, straight away.

Clockwork continuity sales

Some pet businesses naturally lend themselves very well to continuity sales.

Dog walkers and daycare owners, for example, usually have clients who lead consistently busy lives and need regular daycare or walks for their dogs.

Dog groomers also should have clients who should come back every four or six weeks like clockwork.

In fact, unless you are dog walker who loses dogs or a groomer who occasionally sets them on fire, then there is no reason why every client you welcome into your business shouldn't use you regularly and stay clients for a very long time.

Like McDonald's, though, you can't just assume that your clients and customers are going to buy more of your services.

To secure next week's walk, or next month's groom, or that extra training session, you will need to …

…

ASK!

Yep, the key to selling more to your existing clients is simply to offer them more stuff.

You can start with more of the same.

When they purchase a walk or a groom, you need to immediately book them in for the next one. You might even want to give a small discount if they book and pay for the next three months. That's not exactly continuity, but it's three months' guaranteed income, and it's three months when you have effectively locked your clients in, and locked your competitors out.

And dog trainers, massage therapists, hydrotherapists and even pet photographers can get in on the act too. When you do a session with a client, you simply then ask them if they want another one.

There's almost no problem you can attempt to fix for a client that won't be fixed better by booking more sessions. As a trainer, a massage therapist or a hydrotherapist, you can get a better result for your clients by booking in more than one session. Even a pet photographer could get a better range of photographs by doing two sessions instead of one; even if it just means you get to use two locations, the dog will likely be better behaved for you by the second session.

Sell More Stuff Case Study – Karen's Lifetime Customer Value Story

"I have implemented and continue to implement many of the Golden Rules Dominic lays out in this book, and this year one of our main goals was to 'SELL MORE STUFF'. More importantly, to sell that 'more stuff' mainly to the clients I already have, and also to new clients coming on board for just one service.

For example, most clients who sign up for a course struggle with one particular aspect of their dog relationship. The main problem areas for my clients are pulling on lead and not coming back when called.

So this year we have hosted an extra dozen 'Walk Nicely' and 'Come Back' workshops. The income from these workshops is a real bonus, and it now seems crazy to think that we didn't previously try that hard to sell as much as possible to all of the clients we take on board.

Clients book a course with us because they trust us to provide a good service; our main additional aim is to prove we can provide more help for them.

And of course, selling additional services to existing clients is also very cost-effective in terms of marketing, as we don't need to continually spend money finding new clients, and instead simply keep them updated about our up-and-coming events, and point out how they and their dog might find these beneficial."

Karen Boyce
www.beastlythoughts.co.uk

Why keeping quiet will cost you money

Zig Ziglar used to say *"Shy salesmen have skinny kids"*, and if you follow this Golden Rule, you'll soon find that the more you ask, the more you get.

This is something I learned 'in the trenches' when I was a sales rep. I had monthly distribution targets to hit, which meant I had to do A LOT of selling. And selling cold meant I had to take a lot of 'no's before I got the 'yes' I needed.

You, however, *aren't* selling cold. Your clients already know you, and they should be happy with the service you offer. They've already gone through the ***know, like*** and ***trust*** process, and at the moment they aren't looking for anyone else to provide the service you are giving them. This puts you at a tremendous advantage over your competition.

Why you need to sell more to your existing clients

The first cut is the deepest. The first kiss is the sweetest. The first dance is the most awkward and the first sale is the *hardest* one to make. Once you've made that sale, however, and you've converted someone from prospect to customer, then they are the *easiest* people to sell more of your services to.

This *isn't* about fleecing people and selling them stuff they don't want or need. This is about you providing a top-notch service that your clients and their dogs enjoy.

And don't underestimate the power of what you do. In many cases, you are changing lives with your service.

Your dog walking service allows your clients to go to work and not worry about their dog.

Your dog training service removes stress and frustration, keeps dogs and owners together and enriches lives.

Your pet photography or painting service gives your clients the chance to capture forever the essence of their relationship on canvas or print.

Your grooming service enables your clients to enjoy the pleasure of seeing their dog look exactly as they want them too, perfectly clean and pristine.

If you are offering *that* kind of service, and I've no doubt that you are, then why wouldn't you want to give your clients the chance to buy more of your amazing services?

But, I don't have anything else to sell? I hear you cry!

And that is a problem for sure.

The only way to fix that is to *create* more things to sell.

This is something I work very hard on with my private coaching clients, who often go from selling only one thing, a walk, a groom, a training session, etc., to having a whole suite of products and services to offer.

Sell More Stuff Client Case Study – Nick's Continuity Story …

"Like most dog trainers, continuity was a huge problem for me. I saw a client once and then never heard from them again. Thankfully Dom helped me to solve this problem by implementing four-session packages and quadrupling my prices during the time I worked with him. Now I have a system which maximises each customer's lifetime value.

I was able to develop my customer's journey, and with each client I refined both the funnel and my sales approach. Now almost every single client I see opts to pay for four more sessions on my first visit, and we book in our next one there and then.

The new strategy has been so successful I've been able to bring my partner into the business and have had to implement a waiting list.

Dom also encouraged me to resurrect my podcast, which I had sorrily abandoned … and thank god he did. It's now grown to become one of the most popular dog training podcasts available and led to all kinds of new business opportunities, an incredible network and a tonne of personal enjoyment.

The podcast caught the attention of an American television production company and led to a job consulting as a dog expert along with other offers of TV work. This is a whole new stream of income that I may never have ventured into without Dom's invaluable advice."

Nick Benger
www.nickbenger.com

How to upsell your current clients

Let's start with an easy one, and something you can get started with straight away. Sticking with the 'Golden Rules' theme, you can introduce a 'silver service'.

A silver service is the kind of dining you get in fancier and more expensive hotels and restaurants. It's a style of serving food at formal meals in which the server uses a silver spoon and fork in one hand to serve the food item by item on to the diner's plate.

The food isn't really any different to the food you would get anywhere else, but by presenting it in a more formal and fancy way, restaurants can charge more money for the silver service.

So, how can you silver service your offering? Let's take a look.

If you are dog walker who does hour-long walks, then you can add in some scentwork games, call it a Scent-tastic Adventure.

If you are a dog trainer, you could offer bonus Skype calls to deal with ad hoc issues, or group support in a private forum.

Groomers could offer a groom that also includes a teeth clean or a facial for the dog, and call it a top-to-toe make-over.

If you are a pet photographer, you could offer an enhanced indoor/outdoor package, or some bonus blooper shots and video clips that your clients can share on social media.

Straight to silver

Now, not all of your clients are going to buy the upsell version all the time, but many *will*, often straight away. Sometimes they will jump straight to the higher-priced version and skip your base offering altogether.

The key is to offer them more of the same, and offer them the option of a higher-priced, silver service version as well.

You have to offer it, though. Remember, shy salespeople have skinny kids, and empty bank accounts.

As a pet business owner you are salesman too, or a saleswoman, of course. (No gender neutrals here, pick a side please.)

Be proud of your service, shout it from the rooftops and offer more of it to the people who are most likely to buy from you, i.e. your existing clients.

Summary

Each stage of your business journey is exciting and stressful in equal measure, and expanding your business can be as difficult as just starting out. Let's recap the Golden Rules that will allow your business to grow and expand.

Golden Rule Number 4 – Systemise Your Business. Trusting your staff with the precious clients and dogs you've built a relationship with is easier when you have a signature system. Your signature system for delivering your expert service is a template that anyone can follow. It allows you to multiply yourself so you can help more dog owners in your town. It gives your clients confidence that your standards won't slip, and your new staff member will feel like they are entering a professional organisation. You'll see in the next chapter how your 'system' can also be an asset that you can sell elsewhere too.

Golden Rule Number 5 – Sell More Stuff. It's difficult to scale a business that only sells one thing and is always looking for new clients. The easier way to build a sustainable business is **to sell more services** to your *existing clients*, *and*, if possible get them onto some kind of continuity programme where they pay you regularly and consistently, month after month, year after year. You probably have services already that your existing clients would buy if only they knew you offered them, but if you don't then you can start by introducing a 'silver service' version of your existing offering. Some of your clients will upgrade straight away. That means there's money on the table you are missing out on by not offering a higher-priced 'super-dooper' option …

Systemising Your Business and Sell More Stuff Bonus – If you are currently at phase two of your business journey, then as well as systemising your service you'll also need to start systemising your marketing. Email marketing is the best way to follow up online, and to help you get started with email I'm giving you access to my **Email Marketing Crash Course**. In this seven-day email crash course, I will show you in more detail how you can use email marketing as the perfect follow-up to sell more to your existing clients and increase the profitability of your business. To get this course for free, go to **www.growyourpetbusinessfast.com** and click on the free resources tab.

Chapter 4

The Ultimate Pet Business Plan

Phase Three: Innovating, Expanding and Re-inventing an Established Pet Business

Life is full of twists and turns, and it often leads you down unexpected avenues. As an example, I *never* imagined I would be running a dog business when I was a kid. I didn't even own a dog.

When young Dom was a nipper, he wanted to be an actor. Shocked you there, didn't I!

I was 10 years old when my aunt took me along to a local amateur dramatics group. I could sing a little and did a show with them (*The Sound of Music* if you *must* know); then I got the acting bug, and that was all I wanted to do.

I left school at 16 and trained for two years in a local performing arts college. I performed here and there, and sang in pubs and clubs for a few years. Then I met my wife, Beth, and we had a son, Alex, and eventually I got sick of not having enough regular income, so quit the singing and dancing lark to get a 'proper job'.

That was job change number one.

I spent the next 10 happy years as a sales rep, before I eventually got bored of that, and so I hung up my briefcase and started a dog business.

That was job change number two.

So, only two main jobs, but they have been quite different.

The really big changes for me have happened since I *started* my pet business, which has undergone several re-inventions since it began in 2011.

Tinker, tailor, trainer, speaker …

I started out as a dog walker/runner, then I started offering dog adventures, and I transitioned to being a dog trainer in 2013.

Then I become a 'shopkeeper' when I launched an online store in 2015. The store was a disaster, but I learned a lot and had more success launching an online dog training programme in 2016.

Shortly after that, I wrote my first book, *How To Be Your Dog's Superhero.* I built on that success by becoming a prolific author with another four books being launched in the next four years. That led to a successful speaking career.

My podcasts mean I'm a presenter and broadcaster, and the newsletter business means I'm also a publisher. For the last three years I've been a full-time pet business coach and mentor to ambitious dog trainers, walkers and groomers.

What does the future hold for me? It's hard to say right now, but I wouldn't bet against the next seven years being just as eventful.

But, enough about me. This book is about your business and what your future holds.

Now, I'm not suggesting you should do, or even want to do, anything that I've done in my business journey, but if you've been running your business for any length of time, then you should think about how you can evolve, innovate and maybe even completely re-invent your business.

Do you need to re-invent a successful business?

On one hand, no, you don't. If you've created your dream business and are happy to continue doing the same thing day in and day out, then you can continue to do that.

However, if you feel like you are more of an 'entrepreneur' than a business owner, then you may want to evolve your business to prevent you going stale. And even if you *aren't* motivated to try something new at the moment, you should *still* keep an open mind about being innovative in your business, because that will help you identify threats and opportunities, and enable you to stay ahead of the competition.

Which direction to go in?

Many of the pet business owners I mentor who already have an established business usually have a ton of ideas for their future, but no clue how to action them, or which idea to pick first.

My advice is to take your business in the direction you have

a. the most experience in
b. are most interested in
c. can make the most money from.

And despite what you might think, this is *not* the criteria you used when you started your current business.

See, when you began your pet business, you probably had one business idea, and that idea was based on the limited experience you had at the time.

So, you probably had a passing interest in dog training, walking, grooming, massage, photography, etc., but you didn't have much knowledge about the industry as a whole.

At that time you were also transitioning from being an employee to a business owner, which is liberating and exciting, but also difficult *and* stressful. Your main goal when you started your business was to replace your wage as quickly as you could, partly to secure your future (and also so you could justify your decision to start your business in the first place).

You didn't know it, but back then you were viewing the business world through a telescope.

Now, you have in-depth knowledge and more experience of the industry, so you can see the whole picture. Couple that with your experience of actually running a business, and you have a much better idea of what your dream business now looks like, and what changes you need to make moving forward.

Here's an example of how my own dream business developed.

When I started my dog adventure business, I wanted nothing more than to be outside with the dogs every day. And that's exactly what I ended up doing. For two years I worked solid on the business, hardly took a holiday and loved every minute with my adventure dogs.

Then I was full but wanted to grow further, so I took on a member of staff.

I wanted to make more money but had run out of hours in the day, even with a staff member. So, I decided to try a sideways move, which led to me setting up an online store. I thought I could work that side of the business around the dog adventure service. I was wrong about that and ended up hating the online adventure store I'd spent a fortune building. It wasn't a total disaster, though, because that experience taught me if I wanted to grow the business, I would need to master marketing so I could better advertise and promote my new services.

By then, I knew what I liked *and* what I hated about running a business.

I'd successfully taken on a staff member, and I knew I would need staff going forward so I could have some time off, but I also knew I wasn't suited to and didn't want to have lots of staff members. That ruled out the option of rolling out my dog adventure model across the country, as that would mean taking on more and more staff.

Neither did I want to sell toys and treats online. Six months of packaging up parcels and taking them to the post office was enough for me.

I wanted to create a business that allowed me to help more people, earn more money and have an impact, but that was also a low numbers business with regard to staff and inventory.

I did that by writing books and creating courses, something I'll talk about later in this chapter.

So, I built my business around the skills I developed like writing and teaching, and I avoided the big staff numbers that I knew would cause me a headache.

This is not to say that expanding your business and scaling up with staff members, or running an online store, won't be right for you, but for me it wasn't appealing, so I went in a different direction.

What you love *and* hate about your current business are important questions you need to ask *before* you expand.

The last thing you want is to create a bigger beast that swallows up more of your time and effort, and which you don't enjoy.

Is there a perfect time to expand or change direction?

The honest answer to that is 'NO'.

Ideally, you would have a solid business base to build from, but it doesn't always work out that way.

I chose to build my local dog adventure business up to a level I was happy with, then I coasted for a while before I got restless and was ready for a new challenge. The first time I tried to expand I opened an online store, but I didn't have any staff so ended up doing all the extra work myself, which was ultimately very draining, and while it wasn't the main reason my online venture failed, it was certainly a contributing factor.

The second time around I did it the right way, and systemised and staffed the adventure business (the same way I described to you in phase two of this book), which enabled me to concentrate fully on the new direction my business was going in. For me that new direction was about writing, teaching, creating online courses and leveraging my expert dog training and marketing knowledge.

And I'm not the only one to have done this…

Be an Expert Client Case Study – Carol's Re-invention Story …

"Eleven years ago, I retired early from a professional career. Not wanting to sit and do nothing, I turned my dog training hobby into a business. I pottered along for around six years earning no more than pocket money, doing what I'd been doing for years in a dog training club. But I was dissatisfied. I was busy and full up. I wanted to develop my business further and earn more money, but I had no idea how to do it.

Then I came across Dom's 33 business ideas. Gold dust. That led onto a coaching call with Dom as one of his first clients around three years ago. That call changed my life and I joined the newly formed Pet Business Inner Circle.

On Dom's advice, I stopped running the wide range of different classes I was providing so I could focus on the core of the business, which was pet dog training and behaviour. I increased my prices – and I have done another seven times since then, so I now charge over eight times my pre-Dom rates and I'm proudly premium.

I then attended Dom's first dog trainers' Bootcamp. It was an intense experience, unlike any other conference I'd ever been to, and I came away with four full pages of ideas and actions I needed to take. I changed my business to become even more niched and I took on my first assistant. That year I also wrote my first book, *Pesky Puppy to Perfect Pet* (now in its second edition, available from Amazon).

In my second year PD (post-Dom) I wrote my second book, *Chaos to Calmish: Diary of a Pesky Puppy's First Year*, and attended IMPACT, the bigger and better dog trainers' Bootcamp. Again I came away with loads of ideas and actions. I systemised, revamped and re-launched my existing dog training course to provide a system that leads our clients from basic training through real-life practice and onto regular fun classes through a membership programme, our Down Dog Devotees.

At IMPACT again last year, I came away with even more actions and ideas, but the biggest revelation was I finally nailed my niche. At that event, pushed by Dom, I finally realised that my previous career and my current business were actually very similar – and I became The Doggy Doctor.

But I still needed and wanted more. I joined Dom's Platinum group after that event. Before that I thought (correctly) I'd been doing pretty well and I was developing my business fairly quickly and efficiently, but being in Platinum is an exhilarating, exciting, rollercoaster, perpetual challenge.

I've written my third book (*Problem Pooch to Perfect Pet Book 1*, also available from Amazon) and I have books 4, 5 and 6 planned out

I produce a print newsletter every two months for my clients, which also acts as advertising in local vets and pet outlets.

I've revamped the behaviour side of the business into the Doggy Doctor Surgery, where people can book House Visits, and I've also added online Consultation Call options for clients who want that.

I've written, and am currently testing, my first live online course – something I would still be fiddling with trying to get 'right' if Dom hadn't pushed me to 'just do it' – with plans for three more to come next year.

I'm starting to develop a 'business within a business' aimed at newbie dog trainers.

The future is rosy for me!"

Carol Clark – The Doggy Doctor
www.downdog.co.uk

How can your pet business evolve?

With a plan, of course!

The beauty of running your own pet business is you can, with the right plan, go in any direction you want.

Yes, it may take some time to switch from being a dog walker to a dog groomer, or to go from being a local dog trainer to a digital dog trainer who has books, and online programmes, but that's the fun part about being a business owner. You get to decide, and if you've followed the Golden Rules so far, then you'll have a profitable, fun business that allows you to comfortably pay the bills while you build up your knowledge and reputation in the new direction you want to take your business.

And with the marketing skills you have perfected so far, you should find it easier to launch, market, grow and make a profit from the new area of your business.

Money isn't the only factor, of course, but it's the big one. Extra profits allow you to take more time out of the business and treat your family to nice things. That's certainly why I'm in business. Well, that and my love of dogs …

WARNING: I have a word of caution if you are thinking about ditching your current dog business and starting another. Unless you absolutely hate your current business, or are physically unable to do it, then I would always suggest fixing your current business *before* your start another one, and I'll tell you why.

Often when clients come to me and they want to move from being a dog groomer to a dog walker, or they want to move from being a dog walker to a dog trainer, or they want to switch from doing classes and one-to-ones to running online dog training courses, they initially want that because they are sick of their current business. Often this is because they have failed to follow Dom's Seven Golden Rules …

Failure to implement the Seven Golden Rules, or the five I've shared with you so far, usually means they create a business that offers a bazillion services (no niche), charges horrendously low prices (non-premium), has no effective way to communicate with dog owners in their town, which instead means they just mess around on Facebook (no media), they have no time off (no staffing or systemising) and they work long hours offering basic services which bring in low fees (no-upselling), which leads to a pissed-off pet business owner who dreams of setting fire to the whole thing so they can start over doing something else entirely.

The main problem with that is unless you learn how to fix your current business, you will in all likelihood repeat the exact same mistakes in your new business. You might be a little bit happier for a while, but ultimately the new business will have the same problems as the first.

So, make sure that you first fix your current business, or if you really can't stomach another day, then at least identify where you went wrong, so you can start your new business with new principles, *and* a new business plan to help you do things differently this time around.

Having said that, I do think it's a good idea to diversify your income streams so you aren't so dependent on one way of making money.

The great Dan Kennedy says the most dangerous number in business is one.

The loss of one key supplier, your one big customer, your one way of communicating with your prospects, that one main service you offer, can be devastating for your business, and in some cases can even end it.

So, once you've fixed your current business, nailed your niche, are charging considerably more than your competitors, have increased the lifetime customer value of your clients and systemised your services, what should you do next?

Well, one option would be to start offering more complementary services. Dog owners need lots of things from food and training to grooming and doggy daycare, and everything else in between. So, you could create a one-stop shop that offers all of the above, and more.

I have a few private clients who offer such a service in their town, but they are willing to tolerate a lot more pain than I am when it comes to staffing and dealing with clients.

And there are lots of other ways you can diversify and repurpose your business systems without scaling up and overseeing all the work yourself.

Selling your system

The proprietary system you created in phase two is actually a valuable asset you can sell many different ways.

If you have a successful, proven business model, then you could choose to franchise or license that model to new and inexperienced business owners (who are just like you were when you started your business).

By now you've no doubt spent a lot of time and put a lot of effort into practising and perfecting your dog walking, grooming and training systems, and (assuming they work) those systems contain valuable information that someone starting a new pet business will gladly pay money to learn.

Doggy daycare owners could sell their system to other doggy daycare owners who want to 'fast-track' their learning.

Canine massage therapists and hydrotherapists could sell their system to people who are just starting out too.

Selling your system around the world

There's also the option of selling information products and courses around your 'niche' too. This will enable you to scale your business and sell your 'expertise' to dog owners all over the world.

You're probably thinking that this only applies to dog trainers, but you'd be wrong.

For sure, dog trainers are the obvious candidates to create information products, and if you are a dog trainer reading this, then you should definitely be thinking about ways you can leverage all the knowledge you've spent years collecting and practising, by packaging it up and selling it to dog owners who live beyond your 'local' area.

But, dog trainers aren't the only ones who can jump on the information-products bandwagon. If you are a successful dog walker, groomer, pet photographer, massage therapist, or daycare owner, then you *also* have skills that dog owners will gladly invest in.

All this is much easier to do if you followed Golden Rule Number 2 and 'specialised' your service. Remember it's easier to be a big fish in a small pond by creating a dog training course for terriers than it is to just do a 'generic' dog training course suitable for any dog.

You can, if you work at it enough, create a whole other business around your niche that includes books, courses and seminars.

And that nicely leads us to **Golden Rule Number 6 – Be the Expert**, because no matter what direction you want to take your established business, you'll do it better if you are recognised as an authority figure, and that is exactly what writing a book will do for you.

Writing a book, and being recognised as an author, will almost immediately elevate you near the top of your industry. Quite simply, being an author puts you in a very small category of people who have done something as extraordinary as writing a book.

Seriously, people treat you like you've won the Nobel Peace Prize when they find out you are an author.

There are lots of reasons why writing a book will raise your profile and make you someone worth listening to, and you can write a book at any stage of your business journey (phase one or two), but the reason I have it in phase three is it is easier to write and publish a book if you already have a stable business in place.

Assuming you go down the self-publishing route (which is what I've done and would highly recommend), then you will have to pay for the cover, the formatting, the proofreading and the printing itself (and the promotion too).

Yes, this can be done on the cheap, but like anything in life, you get what you pay for, and the last thing you want is a shit-looking book. Trust me, I've seen enough embarrassing, mistake-ridden manuscripts to know that not every dog book doth an expert make.

My suggestion would be to make sure you are financially comfortable before you begin writing your book. Writing a book is a big deal, and it will take you time to complete, so better you tackle this task from a position of comfort in your business.

Be The Expert Client Case Study – Natasja's Niching Story …

"When I first came across Dom, my dog training business was struggling, and I didn't have a clue how to get back on top. I was trying to offer everything I thought my clients wanted. If someone asked me for a class, I would put it on. I ended up with a wide variety of classes and only one or two people in each of them. I wasn't making any money. I tried to do everything, and it wasn't working.

I was scared to niche down and show my potential clients that I was an expert in my field. I was afraid to charge what I knew I was worth as I believed I would be pushing my potential clients to the local competition.

I knew I needed help, not just on the marketing front but also on how to stabilise and grow my business. Dom started by encouraging me to raise my prices, niche down and then talk about my speciality.

It took a lot of courage to niche down. I am so glad Dom kept on at me, encouraging me to do it. What made the most significant difference was establishing a firm foundation. I developed my 'Fun | Focus | Play®' training system and niched down to just one area.

Dom also encouraged me to write my book *No Pulling Allowed*, and this helped to establish my expert status further. He supported and encouraged me and gave invaluable advice during the writing process, making my book the best it could be. The reviews so far have all been very positive, and I know that without Dom's support, I would not have pushed ahead and finished writing it.

I still have a long way to go, but my income has doubled. My business is steadily growing and expanding. I am no longer struggling, and it is all because I followed Dom's advice and became the Dog Walking Expert."

Natasja Lewis
www.nightsabredogtraining.co.uk

Which leads me nicely onto what your book is going to do for you.

What your book will do for you

You should think of your book as a sales tool. And, for your book to 'sell' your service effectively, it needs to contain the four Ps:

Personality – As much as you might think it, the world doesn't need another long, boring book that talks about the history of dog training. Your book needs to be packed with personality and contain stories that will demonstrate what you are teaching, AND they will help you form a bond with the reader.

Problem – Your book should solve a problem for the reader. It should help them to do something. So a dog groomer's book might help the reader to get their puppy used to the groomers, or it might help them to maintain their cockapoo's coat between grooms. It's not hard to find out what your ideal clients' problems are; you just ask them. This means the book also needs to be practical.

Practical – You can't assume your book reader knows (or wants to know) as much about your subject as you do. So, you should make every effort to ensure your book is practical. That means it should be easy to understand, and fol low through with the promises you make in the book's description. Dog trainers find this most difficult, and they end up writing about behavioural quadrants, cues and learning theory, all of which flies over the head of the average pet dog owner.

Purpose – This might surprise you, but your book's purpose isn't actually to make money. Not initially anyway. See, as difficult as it might be to understand, your book probably isn't going to be the next *Harry Potter* and hit the *NY Times* bestseller list. Sorry to burst a bubble. You might make some passive income, all of my books bring in some nice passive income sales, but their main purpose is to bring people into my world. Your book provides a bridge between someone knowing nothing about you to potentially becoming a client.

Follow the four Ps publishing plan and you'll create a book that is entertaining, educational and effortlessly sells your services to the reader.

A very well-known dog training friend of mine told me a story about how she was selling some of my books in her shop when one of her clients asked a question about it. She replied it was a good book and the trainer actually knew the author (me). The client couldn't believe that her trainer (who, I should add, is vastly more qualified and experienced than me) actually knew the author of *How To Be Your Dog's Superhero*. Needless to say, my dog trainer friend realised the power of writing a book and will soon have her own in print.

And you should too.

To help you get started with this, I've included a couple of cool book-writing bonuses; simply head to

www.growyourpetbusinessfast.com/resources to grab yours.

So, writing your book will position you as an expert, and it will also help you with **Golden Rule Number 7 – Be a Leader**.

Once you've decided which new direction you want to take your pet business in, you don't really want to just 'dip your toe in the water' and dabble with the new venture. You should want to make a big splash and quickly convince everyone that you are someone who should be listened to and followed.

And followers need a leader.

I'm not talking about you being a world-famous leader in the *whole* dog industry. There's actually not a lot of benefit to you making yourself famous to everyone. Remember, we are dealing in 'niches'. What you want is to be seen as a 'leader' in a particular niche with your industry.

You might not think of yourself as being 'leadership' material, and for a short while you may have to carry a 'fake it till you make it' attitude, until your confidence catches up with your skills. But, it will do eventually, and you'll get there faster if you follow the strategies below.

Write a book – Yes, I know this is Golden Rule Number 6 repeated, but for a very good reason. Leaders are readers, and leaders are also writers. Don't be someone who just consumes content; be a creator. And there's no better way to stamp your authority in a niche than by writing a book.

Be an educator and a person of influence in your niche – You can easily build up to writing a book by writing blogs, emails and articles. Experts and leaders have opinions about important matters in their industry, so take a stand on topics that you are passionate about. This allows you to build a tribe around you of people who are aligned with your values.

Give interviews – This carries on from the last point, and you should make an effort to get your business featured in the newspaper, radio and magazines. Getting PR will add a celebrity element to your business and make you seem more credible to those who you want to attract into your tribe.

This is exactly what I did when I transitioned from being a dog trainer to being Europe's leading pet business coach.

I wrote a book about my experiences of running a successful dog walking business called *Walk Yourself Wealthy*.

I went on a speaking tour and ran my own business bootcamps.

I also created a ton of educational content that positioned me as an expert, including videos, blogs and a podcast.

I did interviews in the local papers, and radio, and I've been interviewed on other podcasts, all which helped to position me as someone with credibility, authority and a celebrity status. Celebrity status doesn't mean I have paparazzi from *Hello!* magazine outside my house trying to get snaps of me hanging the washing out, but it does mean that I built up my profile as an expert business coach within the 'pet industry', which is *my niche*.

To establish myself as a leader, I did all the things I've told you to do in *The Ultimate Pet Business Plan*.

So, if you are a leader, who will be your followers?

This is why having a niche is so important when it comes to establishing yourself as a leader, and to help me make this point, I need to enlist the help of my Dogue de Bordeaux, Derek.

My wife and I are huge fans of the DDB, and I would imagine we will own at least one for the rest of our lives.

This also means I'm a member of DDB groups on FB, I support DDB charities, and I'll buy stuff that has a DDB on it.

You'll have your own breed you are mad about, and you probably can't understand why I love DDBs so much.

That's OK, though; you *don't* need to share my doggy passion, and I *don't* need to share yours.

But, you need to understand that 'the dog world' as a single entity doesn't really exist.

It's a universe of different doggy planets.

A collection of connected but distinctive doggy niches. And those of you who are planning to make a kind of name for yourself in this industry, and create another 'business within your current business', will do well to plant a flag on one of those planets, position yourself as a leader and expert, find out what their pain points are, and THEN sell them your stuff.

The stuff you sell them will obviously be 'breed' or 'niche' specific. And as we learned in phase one, you can charge more for 'niche specific' advice than you can for just regular dog training advice (EVEN THOUGH IT'S BASICALLY THE SAME ADVICE!).

In a way, Golden Rule Number 7 – Be a Leader – is a development of Golden Rule Number 2 – Be Specialised. Only this time, instead of choosing a niche, you are now claiming a niche. You are establishing yourself as a leader and authority figure within that niche.

Be a Leader Client Case Study – Claire's Business Regeneration Story …

"I always knew that what I was doing back then wasn't fulfilling my potential. I had a drive to go further, but no clue of how to get there. I started the business, leaving a full-time head chef job, walking dogs. Moving on to offering more services than I care to remember. I was running out of time and energy every day and quickly.

I qualified as a dog trainer and started offering basic training on the walks. I soon found that although this made our jobs easier and more fulfilling, the owners weren't doing the work needed to maintain what we'd been teaching. I had staff back then, and every Monday lunchtime, we'd all say the same thing.

'We're back to square one again with the training after the weekend.'

It pissed me off, and that's when I started thinking about getting rid of the business. Either starting again or just going back to employment. It wasn't just the owners not doing the work; other factors were involved and I totally fell out of love with what I was doing.

I came across Dom and decided to give it one last try. It couldn't hurt to see what was on offer, though I was sceptical and cautious all the same. What could some guy do that was going to make me A: get out of the hole I'd got myself into and B: love my business again.

Turns out a lot actually. From being a local dog trainer (who nobody really knew much about), I've transformed into a digital dog trainer, who's also an author and who people are quite literally raving about.

I got stopped at the petrol station with 'Ooh, you're High Peak Dogs, aren't you?' and another one at the car garage: 'I've heard great things about you.'

It freaked me out a bit at first, but I'm now being recognised locally for my skills and the quality of service I bring. What's equally as great is I'm not busting my ass every day to get around everyone. I went from 33 clients, with no time, limited money left for myself after staff and no energy because I was still working around the clock to put food on the table, down to the 12 clients who worship me when I come through the door. I have more time available to me than I've ever imagined possible, and the clients continue to use me through the school holidays even when home and pay me when they go off on their jolly holidays. But more importantly, they do the homework I set them and are the kind of people I like working with.

Dom helped me to fix the current business, nail my niche, charge prices I viewed as a telephone number and give me more quality time for myself.

My clients are worth just as much to me as the 33 I did have. All with better training results. They get a service unlike any other around here with monthly mail, gifts and a community they enjoy.

So, I've become premium, specialised, write daily to my tribe, created my own courses and media, and I have systemisation in place. I sell more to my existing clients. I still don't feel like an expert, but I've written two books on barking dogs, and I am being viewed as one by others. I'm also a leader, running events and seminars, and my clients look to me for advice, support, queries, etc.

I've attracted and continue to attract my ideal clients. I'm building profits and getting more referrals now than ever. I had to take on a VA to assist with the influx of emails and application forms from people wanting to work with me.

Out of the 100% out there, I wanted to be and am in that 5%. When I get told to go out and do the fucking work, I go out there and do the fucking work. That's why I've transformed my business. I love it and am continuing to thrive, all for a better life."

Claire Lawrence
www.highpeakdogservices.co.uk

The world is more connected than it's ever been, and the power of the internet has made it possible and easier than ever for you to establish yourself as an influencer, educator and leader in a niche.

Do you want to become known as the world's foremost pet photographer who specialises in taking aquatic shots of water-loving gundogs? You can do that.

Do you want to establish yourself as the leading female dog trainer who helps older people find and train a dog they can enjoy in their old age? You can do that.

Are you a groomer who has a deep passion for grooming the bichon frise? You can become a world-renowned expert in that frise field!

Are you a dog walker who is passionate about poodles and want to start a dog owning association for cockapoo, labradoodle and other poo-loving owners? You can do that.

Do you run a doggy daycare that specialises in providing much-needed help for owners who have recently adopted a rescue dog? You can become a leader in that field.

When it comes to evolving and re-inventing your pet business, it is about stripping away the things you don't want (or no longer enjoy doing), and instead forging a pathway that goes a mile deep into a particular niche.

Be a Leader Client Case Study – Katie's Rescue Dog Story …

"My business wasn't broken; it was new, exciting, almost fully booked every day; I had lots of ideas, plots, schemes, inspiration and goals to make it even better. Far from broken, it was working great … just not for me. As well as running two secure fields, I was full time at Dogs Trust. I had all of these ideas brewing but no time to implement them. I was frustrated, burning out.

My mission in life has always been to help those dogs most in need, and at Dogs Trust I was doing that. On the other hand Dogwood allowed me the creative freedom I craved

– but I felt uneasy about leaving the world of rescue and going private.

I was conflicted. How could I create a business that was fun and worked for me yet was profitable enough to support charities and help rescue dogs? I needed help. Cue Dom.

I joined PBIC early 2018 and became a Platinum client shortly after the IMPACT event.

In the six short months that I have been a client, Dom has helped me nail down my niche, and create a signature system that is scalable and sellable and has established Dogwood as a business of influence.

Most importantly, we have created an income that allows us to support rescues and the dogs in their care. We donate regular sessions to local rescues, provide reduced-price play sessions to the families of newly adopted rescue dogs and carry out several fundraising events throughout the year.

One such event was Open Fields Day in September 2019, where we welcomed over 600 people through our gates and raised in excess of £1,200 for local charities in four hours.

Those figures aren't possible to achieve alone. Changing the world can't be done single-handedly. The success of the events I've organised was due to the quality and quantity of the people who wanted to be involved. I've cultivated a strong support network of local businesses – dog trainers, walkers, groomers, shops specialising in canine wares, dog photographers, hydrotherapy centres – that come together to help achieve the vision of a better world for dogs and their owners.

Every week, I receive emails, messages and phone calls from other field owners setting up businesses. I've started a consultation service to help enable them to achieve their dreams too. This means I'm indirectly helping dogs across the whole country (our website copy has even turned up on an American dog park site! While I'm not a fan of copycats, this was pretty impressive!).

Most days we receive messages from clients, photos of their happy dogs enjoying our playgrounds, telling us how Dogwood has changed their lives, how they weren't sure whether they could keep their dogs as their lives were a nightmare but because they're finally able to relax they've rekindled their relationship, first-time-off-lead-stories, tears-in-the-eyes stories.

This is just the beginning. Dom has helped me look ahead; we play the long-game now."

Katie Guastapaglia

Canine Enrichment Officer – Dogwood Adventure Play
www.dogwoodadventureplay.com

The advice I've given in this third phase of the pet business journey is deliberately less prescriptive than in the first two phases.

The reason is I want you to feel free to go in whatever direction you desire.

However, when you are starting and growing a business, I firmly believe, and my clients' results confirm, that you should always aim to

1. Be Premium
2. Be Specialised
3. Create Your Own Media
4. Systemise Your Business
5. Sell More Stuff

That's the first five Golden Rules, which are the foundations of a successful, sustainable and scalable pet business.

Golden Rules 6 and 7 show you how to build on that dream business in a way that keeps you engaged, interested and excited, and it allows you to get the respect, recognition and the financial rewards your experience deserve.

Golden Rule Number 6 – Be the Expert. By phase three of your business journey you should certainly feel like an expert, and it's likely you know as much, or more, than any of your competitors. Writing a book that is full of personality, which solves a problem for the reader, will position you as that expert in your niche. Certainly, none of your competitors will have written a book. Your book cements your expert status and is the catalyst for the new direction of your business.

Golden Rule Number 7 – Be a Leader. It's likely you've lost some focus and picked up a lot of 'excess baggage' over your years in business. Like services you offer but don't enjoy delivering, which you introduced because a client requested them and you didn't want to upset them. Do this a lot and you can end up with a business that is profitable, but unfulfilling for the business owner, i.e. you! The trick is strip away all the things you don't enjoy and double down on the topic you are uber passionate about.

Being a leader is not about shouting and screaming about your expertise. It's about pulling together all of the skills and experiences you have built up over the years, and distilling them all into positioning you as a leader and expert within a narrowly defined niche within the pet industry.

Be a Leader Client Case Study – Rachel's New Business Story …

"First up, I'm not a pet professional. I'm a pet journalist and blogger and signed up for Dominic's emails after chatting about his first book.

After about six months of hearing him telling people they should write books, I thought, 'I can do this.'

When I launched my blog, a lot of businesses got in touch asking about how to get press coverage. I would email tips back and forth or share them on the phone.

As a journalist writing almost exclusively about pets, I knew my niche, what editors wanted and what stories petpreneurs should be sharing, so I figured, why not put it into a book?

It transformed my business. It gave me more authority than I'd had as one of thousands of journalists.

Since writing it, I've run successful coaching programmes helping pet businesses with blogging and publicity and worked 1–1 with clients (including Dominic), helping them secure coverage in newspapers, magazines, TV shows and on the radio.

I've spoken at events, been able to pretty much stop doing work I didn't like and my hourly rate has quadrupled.

Yes, it was a hassle to take a month away from my regular work to write my book, and a leap of faith, but it paid off."

Rachel Spencer
www.publicityforpetbusinesses.co.uk

Book-writing Bonus – I appreciate writing a book can seem a little daunting, so I have a special bonus that will kickstart your book-writing process. Remember, this is the book that will catapult you above the competition, cement your expert status and establish you as a leader in your field. 'Why your book is the best business card' is a one-hour audio training I did with top copywriter and book coach Vicky Fraser. Vicky and I talk about how you can write a book that will position you as the go-to pet professional in your town. To get access to this audio, go to **www.growyourpetbusinessfast.com** and click on the free resources tab.

Chapter 5

How far can you take your business?

In this book, I've given you the key foundations that will help you better position your business so you can quickly be seen as the premier pet business in your town (and if you agree, then please leave a review on Amazon for me).

What's next for you?

Marketing, much like dog training, is not a one-hit wonder, and you can't expect to learn everything you need to know in one book or course. I myself continue to invest in my marketing AND my dog training knowledge. Although it's the marketing training which makes me more money.

And there's a lot more for you to learn.

To have a truly successful sales machine that is constantly bringing in new leads so you never have to suffer the feast and famine flow of clients, you *also* need to know:

- How to identify and attract your ideal client.
- How to build products and offers that your clients will buy.
- How to use referrals to grow your business.
- How to increase the range of products and services you have to offer so you can extract maximum value from every prospect who you turn into a client.
- How to build continuity into your business so you have more regular and predictable income.
- How to automate your marketing and systemise your business so you can scale and grow beyond your current location – or even just how to take more time off

to enjoy other aspects of your life, relaxed in the knowledge that your business is still ticking over and growing, even while you are not there to oversee everything.

So if you want it, then there's a lot more to learn, and to help you I have some in-depth free training for you to enjoy.

Yes, free.

See, it's not enough for me that you've bought this book. I want you to action it.

You need to action it.

The very future of your pet business depends on how many of Dom's Seven Golden Rules you implement.

The easy option is to say all of this is too difficult and go back to how you were marketing your business before, i.e. messing around on social media.

Well, I'm not sorry to say that option is doomed to failure.

When I teach my seminars round the UK, I start by telling the audience that 80% of the people in the room unfortunately won't do anything with the information I'm going to provide.

They will say it's too difficult, or their fear of change will stop them taking action.

You see, 15% of the room will action *some* of what they learn. They will increase their prices, lean into a niche, stop wasting time on Facebook and actually create their own media. These people often usually double their income within a year.

Then there's the 5% who will do most of what I teach them. They usually completely transform their business and end up positioning themselves as the leaders and experts who create a whole new arm of the business. You've read case study examples throughout the book.

The interesting thing is, you get to decide which group you want to be in.

Do you want to run an average or an extra-ordinary pet business?

If it's the latter, then head to the URL below and I'll help you take the next steps on your journey.

Go to **www.growyourpetbusinessfast.com** and click on the free resources tab.

MY FREE GIFT TO YOU

Claim five powerful and profit-boosting free gifts now

I want this book to represent a new start for your pet business.

Like you, I've read loads of books but most of them get shelved as soon as I've finished. In my life there have only been a dozen or so books that I've enjoyed enough for me to want to read them again. More importantly, I've only read a handful of books that have inspired me to take action on the content once I'd finished.

I want this to be one of those books for you, and my mission now is to get you to take action on what you have learned in *The Ultimate Pet Business Plan.*

Your business should be too important to you not to take action and start implementing the marketing secrets I have shared with you. I know for a fact (because I have done it myself) that you will be making more money a lot faster once you actually start.

So to help you get started, I have five special gifts for you.

1. **Gift Number 1** is the full unedited audio version of this book, but you get more than me just reading *The Ultimate Pet Business Plan* . In this exclusive audio I also go off topic and add in even more secrets and examples that show you how you can master all three phases of your pet business journey. You can get immediate access to this amazing

bonus by going to **www.growyourpetbusinessfast.com** and clicking on the free resources tab.

2. **Gift Number 2** is an hour-long Premium Pricing Masterclass that has only ever been seen by members of my 'Pet Business Inner Circle'. It will help you increase your prices without losing clients and help you better deal with objections from price buyers. To get exclusive access to this powerful training, go to **www.growyourpetbusinessfast.com** and click on the free resources tab.

3. **Gift Number 3** will help you kickstart your book-writing process. This is the book that will catapult you above the competition and cement your expert status. 'Why your book is the best business card' is a one-hour audio training I did with top copywriter and book coach Vicky Fraser. Vicky and I talk about how you can write a book that will position you as the go-to pet professional in your town. To get access to this audio, go to **www.growyourpetbusinessfast.com** and click on the free resources tab.

4. **Gift Number 4** is an email marketing crash course. When I do my seminars and events, I always get questions about email marketing. In this seven-day email crash course, I will show you in more detail how you can use email marketing as the perfect follow-up to turn your prospects into clients and grow your dog walking business, fast! To get this course, go to **www.growyourpetbusinessfast.com** and click on the free resources tab.

5. **And the fifth and final gift** is a free subscription to my monthly paper-and-ink newsletter, 'The Pack Leader Business Gazette'. This profitable publication is essential reading for any ambitious pet professional. If you bought the

book direct from me, then you will already be added to my mailing list, but if you are reading the Kindle version, listening to the audio book or got this book as a gift, then you can sign up today and I will mail this monthly business-building newsletter to you, for free. To activate your free subscription, go to **www.growyourpetbusinessfast.com** and click on the free resources tab.

You have in your hands a blueprint for success. There really is no excuse for you not to take one (or all) of these free resources to further build on what you have learned so far. The information in each one of these free gifts has the power to transform your business, but if you implement all of them, you have the potential to put your business growth on steroids.

How far you take your dog walking business is up to you. Is this going to be a hobby business that just pays the bills, or will it be the premium, profitable and fun pet business empire you want it to be?

To get the answer to that question and more help from me, go to **www.growyourpetbusinessfast.com** and click on the free resources tab.

If you have trouble accessing any of these resources, then email Beth at hello@packleaderdogadventures.co.uk and she will be happy to sort it out.

Thanks for reading.
Keep it unreal.
Dom Hodgson

ACKNOWLEDGMENTS

The Ultimate Pet Business Plan is my fifth book overall and the second I've written this year.

You know all about my business story by now, and you'll know it's been full of ups and downs, but overall I've had way more successes than failures.

That is partly down to my 'get shit done' attitude, but it's also due to the company I keep, and the people I surround myself with. That leads me to the next bit of advice I have for you.

Don't let anyone tell you that you can't do anything with your business. If you surround yourself with negative people who drag you down like crabs in a bucket, then it's time to get some new friends.

The great Jim Rohn said *"You are the average of the five people you spend most of your time with"*, and the quickest way for you to 'level up' your thinking and your attitude to success is to start hanging around with people who have achieved, or who are achieving, the kind of things you want to with your business.

I have an awesome team around me, and I wouldn't be here with them, so here's my acknowledgments to the people who help me keep moving forward.

First and always first comes my family.

Beth, my beautiful wife, is by my side in everything I do, and I wouldn't get half (or even a quarter) of it done without her constant support. Toby and Alex are the best boys a dad could ask for and always make me proud (we have a great laugh, too).

Alex also does an amazing job as the Adventure Operations Manager running Pack Leader Dog Adventures, which is the adventure and boarding side of our business. He is ably assisted by Lucy, our Canine Fulfilment Officer, who also takes care of the grooming clients.

My Mam and Dad are always there to help me and Beth with the kids, dogs and the business, so thanks again to you two. X

Thanks also to my good friend and resident expert for all things video, Alex 'the video guy' Wardle. Alex takes care of all my podcasts, events and online training videos, and I can't recommend him enough. Go to **www.artifactmedia.co.uk** for more details.

Thanks also to my good friend and 'get shit done' buddy, the brilliant book writing coach, Vicky Fraser. Check out **www.moxiebooks.co.uk**

Thanks also to the wonderful Julia Brown of Brown Owl Design, who, I'm sure you agree, has designed another, rather splendid book cover. Thank you, Julia.

Thanks to Nick Jones from Full Media for proofreading this and my other books.

Huge thanks to my tribe of loyal, kick-ass pet business owners and private coaching clients inside the Pet Business Inner Circle. You guys rock!

And finally, thanks to you, my friend, for buying and reading this book!

OK, you are done. This is the end.

Well, not quite, because now you need to turn the page and claim your free gifts, which will help you plug all this positioning training into your own business.

Remember, to get full and immediate access to the full audio version of this book (including bonus unedited material), go to
www.growyourpetbusinessfast.com/resources

ABOUT THE AUTHOR

Dom Hodgson is an expert dog trainer, bestselling author and Europe's leading pet business coach.

With his eldest son, Alex, he runs the UK's number-one dog adventure company, Pack Leader Dog Adventures. Since 2011, PLDA has been helping dog owners in Sunderland have more fun and less stress with their dogs.

In 2016, Dom wrote the bestselling *How To Be Your Dog's Superhero*, which is available to buy from Amazon Kindle, as an audiobook on Audible or you can get a signed copy (and a special free gift) by going to **www.mydogssuperhero.com/getcopy**

This was followed by *Walk Yourself Wealthy*, *Worry Free Walks* and *The Perfect Puppy Project.*

The Ultimate Pet Business Plan is the second pet business book in the 'Grow Your Pet Business FAST!' series. To find out more about Dom's other books, courses and pet business coaching, you should go to **www.growyourpetbusinessfast.com**

Dom is an international speaker and teaches pet dog owners how to have more fun (and get more control) with their dogs, and pet business owners how to have more fun (and make more money) in their business.

To enquire about booking Dom to speak at an event, you should email Beth on hello@packleaderdogadventures.co.uk

Dom lives in Town Farm with his wife, Beth, youngest son, Toby, and their two dogs, Sid the Cocker and Derek the Dogue de Bordeaux.

Other Books by the Author

Dog Training Books

How To be Your Dog's Superhero – Transform your dastardly dog using the power of play

Other Books in the Street-Smart Dog Training Series (1–3)

Worry Free Walks – How to transform your difficult, dangerous and devilish dog into a problem-free pooch that you're proud to take to the park

The Perfect Puppy Project – The ultimate no-mess, zero-stress, step-by-step guide to raising the perfect puppy

The Hungry Games – Discover how you can bin the bowl and use food to play, train and entertain your perfect pet dog

Pet Business Books

Walk Yourself Wealthy – The quick, easy and no-BS guide to transform your passion for pooches into an insanely profitable and fun dog walking empire

The Ultimate Pet Business Plan – How to launch, grow and scale an outrageously profitable, impactful and fun pet business that dominates your local town

Printed in Great Britain
by Amazon

50885292R00078